J. L. Llewellyn.

Take
My Word
For It

FRANK MUIR & DENIS NORDEN

Take My Word For It

Still more stories from 'My Word!'
a panel game devised by
Edward J Mason & Tony Shryane

 EYRE METHUEN LONDON

First published in 1978
by Eyre Methuen Ltd
11 New Fetter Lane, London, EC4P 4EE

Printed in Great Britain by
Richard Clay (The Chaucer Press), Ltd,
Bungay, Suffolk

ISBN 0 413 38710 0

The pun: two strings of thought tied by an acoustic knot

Arthur Koestler

The puns which are most entertaining are those which will least
bear an analysis

Charles Lamb

Contents

A snapper-up of unconsidered trifles

Shakespeare
The Winter's Tale, Act IV, Sc. 2

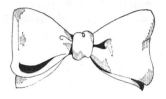

I never really liked Manby.

When he first came to the village I left a card, of course. Actually I got the cards mixed in my pocket and the one I pushed through his door was a Council card saying 'Your cesspool has been emptied' but you know what I mean. I tried.

There was something about the man. Many well-to-do people have a touch of the cilious in their make-up but Manby was supercilious. Although a contemporary of mine, he had a bland, unwrinkled face with a delicate, pink complexion which tempted one to think that he ate babies. And he always seemed to wear those immensely thick tweed jackets with lumps in the tweed, as though it was woven from marmalade.

Matters rather came to a head when he invited me to dinner. He greeted me affably enough.

"What are you taking for it?" he asked.

I fingered the spot on my nose and said, "Well, actually I'm just keeping off fatty things and hoping it will go away."

He closed his eyes in a tiny expression of exasperation.

"That's a figure of speech. What do you want to *drink*?"

"Oh," I said. "I'll have the same as you're having. Pink gin, isn't it?"

"No. Actually it's gin-and-tonic but I cut my finger with the opener."

It was that sort of evening.

He had managed to get hold of some fresh salmon. This was followed by a reasonably decent Tournedos Rossini and a fine wedge of Stilton.

I had a poached egg.

9

Afterwards we settled down in his comfortable study, whose window, he pointed out to me, faced the sea. As the sea was forty-two miles away I thought this point irrelevant but nodded civilly. He helped himself to a brandy-and-soda from a bottle of brandy-and-soda on the desk while I drew on my cigar.

"What are you drawing on your cigar?" he suddenly asked.

I put down my ball-point guiltily.

"Just doodling," I mumbled. "A pin-man riding a bicycle."

He sighed. Reaching for a miniature score of Beethoven's Ninth Symphony he began to turn the pages, his damp lips moving as he silently hummed the first violin part.

After some ninety minutes of this he snapped the book closed, as though he had come to a decision, and looked straight at me.

"I have come to the conclusion, Muir," he said, "that you are something of a charlatan."

"Me?" I said. "A Chinese detective?"

"Not a Charlie Chan – a *charlatan!*" he said, the note of exasperation again creeping in. "A fake. Not what you purport to be. You are supposed to be quick-witted. When, I ask you man to man, were you last quick-witted in my presence. Eh? Eh?"

"Ah," I said, playing for time. Mind racing. "There was an occasion eight years ago when *you* said, 'My housekeeper is putting up fourteen pounds of gooseberry jam' and *I* said, without a moment's pause for thought, 'Up where?'."

His severe expression did not diminish. "I will go further," he said. "In that wireless programme 'My Word!' you pretend to know something of literature and you give the impression that you can play with words on the spur of the moment. It is my belief, after studying you for some years, that they are all written down for you beforehand, probably by some ghost-writing hack in your employ." He paused for effect. "It is my belief that you couldn't ad-lib pussy."

That stung. I rose to my feet, flinging away the ball-point and the remains of the cigar, which now looked like the over-tattooed forefinger of a Maori chieftain.

"Five pounds says I can!" I cried.

"Done," he said. He closed his eyes in thought for some minutes. "I will wager you five pounds that you cannot make a list of the contents of my greenhouse and turn it into a quotation from Shakespeare."

Five minutes later saw us in the greenhouse, he with a torch, me with a pad and pencil.

The first thing the torch lit up was a stuffed bird with a long beak.

"Right," I said. "Shove that old gin bottle next to it and I'm there. 'Now is the woodcock near the gin'. *Twelfth Night.*"

"It isn't a woodcock," he said.

"A teal, perhaps?" I said. "'The Winter's Teal'?"

"It's a snipe."

We moved on. The next object in the torch's beam was a frame thing with wires stretched across it.

"Got it," I said. "That thing is used for riddling top-soil. Lean a hoe against it and you have Goneril's famous line from *King Lear* 'O, ho, I know the riddle!'."

"I haven't got a hoe," he said, "and that isn't a riddle. It's a harp, a Welsh harp. I keep it here because it is warm and the thing won't warp."

"That thing next to it in a pot?" I asked, trying to ignore a slight feeling of desperation gripping my vitals, "Would it by any happy chance be a nut tree? Then when it begins to produce we will have 'Twelfth Nut'?"

"It's a maidenhead fern."

We moved on again. The beam lit up another potted something-or-other.

"Stop!" I said. "If that's a rose, and one of the branches comes from below the surface and is a sport, I'm home and dry – 'Out, damned sport, out, out, I say!' *Macbeth.*"

"It isn't a rose. I'll give you a clue. It's edible."

"Wheat!" I said. "'A rose by any other name will smell as wheat'. *Romeo and Juliet.*"

"It's corn-on-the-cob."

Defeat was staring me in the face. The fat, complacent Manby with his horrible greenhouse-cum-junkyard was going to get the better of me unless I had a bit of luck. And quickly.

I searched the gloom desperately for a bit of greenery that would fit a line of Shakespeare but it all looked the same to me.

I tried to work backwards from Shakespeare. Any pig-swill about so that I could claim 'All's Swill That Ends Swill'? Not one dollop.

Mustard and cress? 'Troilus and Cressida'? Not a leaf.

Green peppers for 'Curryolanus'? Nary a one.

Flowers? 'The Two Gentlemen of Veronica'? It was mid-winter.
A pair of pruning shears? 'Julius Scissor'?
Twine? 'The Rope of Lucrece'?
"Those seed trays!" I found myself shouting hysterically. It was my last chance. "Those trays are full of seed potatoes, aren't they? AREN'T THEY? And there you have it! Potatoes! 'Taters Andronicus'? Or, if you prefer, 'Masher for Masher'? I can even give you a line quotation, 'The quality of murphy is not strained'. I claim my five pounds, sir!"

He smiled a really nasty smile.

"They are lettuce seedlings."

I had lost. The unspeakable Manby had humbled me. But had he? As he turned to leave the greenhouse I happened to glance down at the list of items which I had jotted down and, by thunder, they *did* make up a quotation from Shakespeare!

A snipe.

A harp.

A fern.

Corn.

Seeded trayfuls.

'Take a Pair of Sparkling Eyes'

W. S. Gilbert
'The Gondoliers'

IT began when my son had one of his sore throats. While he was in the bathroom gargling I heard frantic feet thudding down the stairs, then in rushed Glinka, the au-pair girl. I use the word 'girl', but she was actually a middle-aged lady from Lapland who, prior to coming to live with us, had never left her little wooden hut in the northernmost part of Sweden. "The male child!" she shouted, yanking me to my feet, "Happen he's choking of hisself! Send for t'hospital sledge!"

Here I'd better explain that instead of learning her English at the Institute, Glinka was trying to pick it up by studying *Coronation Street*. "Coom quick!" she shouted. "The first-born! Likely he's snoofing it!"

I pelted up to the bathroom, Glinka yelping at my heels. There I found my son standing with his face up-tilted, noisily rolling salt water round the back of his throat. "Hallo, Dad," he said. "Grrrrrr. . . ." Glinka clutched at me desperately. "Do summat!" she pleaded. "Fetch folk from Rover's Return!"

"Oh, give over, Glinka," I said, "he's only gargling." There was a pause. "Doing what?" she said.

"Gargling," I said. "He's having a gargle."

She looked at me with absolute incomprehension. "Gargle?" she said. "What's yon?"

And then it was that a strange anthropological difference between our two cultures came to light. The people of Lapland do not gargle. Whether it's because the clean Arctic air protects them from sore throats or simply that seal-milk is too viscid for tracheal glugging, I don't know. All I can tell you is, Glinka had never before seen anybody performing this commonplace oral activity.

She was completely fascinated. "Show me again," she said to my son. Obediently he took another mouthful of warm salt-water. "Grrrrrr. . . ."

Her eyes shone with wonder. "Can anybody do it?" she said. "Or do you 'ave to belong to an industrialised society?"

"Have a go," I said, handing her the tumbler. She took a generous sip, tilted her head back and imitated my son's noises. Together we leapt at her, he thumping her back while I pushed her head over the washbasin. "Not quite, Glinka," he said. "Very nearly but not quite. The one essential thing to remember is – you must keep your mouth *open*."

Her next attempt was a success. And when she spat out, you should have seen the look on her face. Exhilarated isn't the word. Well, just imagine what it must feel like at the age of forty-three to discover that your body is capable of making a completely new noise! "Here, lad," she said, handing me the tumbler. "Giss a top-oop."

And from then on, there was no stopping her. Not a day passed that we didn't hear her up there in the bathroom emitting her throbbing "Grrrrrr . . .", followed by chuckles of delight. No longer did she spend her free time at wine and reindeer-cheese evenings at the Anglo-Lapland Club. Henceforth, every moment of leisure found her over the washbasin with our cruet and a pint tankard that the children bought her.

Well, it was such a harmless form of diversion and she derived so much inexpensive pleasure from it, it might well have continued for the rest of her sojourn with us. But six months later Britain was suddenly plunged, as seems to happen so frequently nowadays, into one of its periodic consumer crises. This time it was, of all things, a salt shortage. Overnight, every form of table-salt disappeared from the supermarket shelves and the Prime Minister found himself on yet another fast plane to Brussels. ('P.M. To Meet E.E.C. For Salt Talks.') What I was faced with, though, was the uncomfortable fact that if my household's fried chips were to retain any vestige of flavour, Glinka must sacrifice her uvula trilling.

I broke it to her as gently as I could. "I'm sorry, Glinka – but we just can't spare it any more. At a time like this, using salt for leisure-gargling is like people in wartime using petrol for inessential journeys."

I would not have thought it possible for a countenance whose component parts were so flattened to take on such a downcast expression. My son was so moved by it, he forgot to help himself to his sister's chips. "Dad," he said, "couldn't Glinka flavour her lukewarm water with something else? What about all that stuff in the spice-rack?"

Our kitchen featured a spice-rack which my daughter had purchased in Camden Market because she thought the jar labelled Cinnamon might have belonged to the author of the Maigret stories. In the jars were thyme, nutmeg, basil, oregano and something called Cumin Seed which always put me in mind of a Yorkshireman inviting you to enter his house.

After dipping a finger in each, Glinka opted for the nutmeg. "Right gradely," she said and took it upstairs. Moments later, the familiar outboard-motor noises were once more drifting down.

Now comes the peculiar bit. Over the next four weeks we became aware of a distressing change in Glinka. Not only did it manifest itself in the way she performed her duties – mashing the potatoes with the sink-plunger, scouring the saucepans with a left-over hamburger – but her whole demeanour took on aspects of the slatternly, not to say sluttish. Almost, at times – the leering. I thought at first she might just be going through the change-of-climate, but when we finally persuaded her to see a doctor, another astonishing item of scientific information emerged.

Did you know that nutmeg is a mild intoxicant? Absolute fact – especially when taken in quantity. And having laced her gargle-water with it every day for the preceding month, quantity was certainly what Glinka had been taking it in. Not to mince words, she'd spent the whole of the past four weeks smashed out of her mind.

I know that when it's told as baldly as that, the story may arouse scepticism. But I do possess medical confirmation of it. Still available for inspection at any time during working hours is the doctor's curt note ordering us to prise Glinka away from the nutmeg. Just five words – six if hyphens don't count:

'Take au-pair off gargling spice.'

Where my caravan has rested

Edward Teschemacher

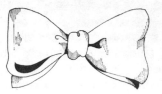

Yesterday afternoon, whilst gazing out of the window at the grass growing, I suddenly felt in urgent need of a walnut and a pair of braces. The ginger cat from next door was in amongst the dahlias.

The walnut was easy to find. There was one left over from Christmas, a perfect missile liable to explode with green dust on impact with the target. The firing mechanism, i.e. the pair of braces, was another matter. Where had I last seen a pair of braces about the house? For that matter, *when* had I last seen a pair of braces? As a *de rigueur* item of gents' outfittery they had gone out about the same time as sock-suspenders, long underwear and semi-stiff detachable collars.

The cat had by now trodden the dahlias flat and was eating a rhododendron. Swift action was called for.

It seemed to me that the likeliest place to find a pair of braces was the cupboard-under-the-stairs, if only because everything which became obsolete, unloved or broken ended up there.

I rushed into the cupboard and was suddenly overwhelmed by a feeling, a sensation difficult to describe, not at all unlike bashing the top of my head against the gas meter.

When I recovered consciousness I switched the light on, made sure the gas meter was still clicking away undamaged and settled down to a leisurely inspection of the contents of the cupboard. The diminution of any sense of urgency came about when I realised that I had closed the door behind me and cupboards-under-the-stairs can only ever be opened from the outside. And my wife was not due home for another three hours.

There were the usual household treasures stacked against the wall; one left gumboot, a pile of *Radio Times* (circa 1948), a lidless tin of rock-hard green paint, a framed steel-engraving of Lord Roberts with the glass broken, a box containing nine dominoes, a gerbil cage (did we keep gerbils? Oh yes, when the children were children. The gerbils produced babies every fortnight which looked like baked beans), a hula hoop (not enough room in the cupboard to prove that my old skill had not left me), the frame of a deck-chair, two-and-a-half pairs of flippers covered with dried sand, an electric kettle of early design minus its element and cord, four Chianti bottles badly converted into reading lamps, a pile of old 78 rpm records (the only one unchipped was The Two Leslies singing 'Oh Monah'), approximately one third of a bicycle, a school satchel (clearly labelled 'P. J. Muir, Form 1b. Touching this is punishable by death'), four home-made lampshades which should have gone on the Chianti bottles but didn't fit, a cushion which the dog had been sick on, a galvanised iron bucket with a hole in the bottom and an early edition of *Radiant Motherhood*.

By the time I had pored over and played with those relics of the past, which at today's inflated prices for items of nostalgia must represent capital of at least 80p, I had worked my way into the sharp end of the cupboard where the lower stairs and the floor came to a point. Here I found an old suitcase wedged. I crawled forward on my knees, levered it free and opened it.

How the memories flooded back as I gazed down on the strange contents within! Here, carefully stored, were the inventions with which I had been going to make my fortune all those years ago. The brilliant devices I had made to fill the long-felt wants of society and make me stinking rich.

Reverently, I reached down and pulled out the top item. This was a round pad, about four inches in diameter, stuffed with feathers and covered in satin. Sewn to one edge of the pad was a six-inch circle of knicker elastic. On the opposite edge was sewn a fisherman's lead weight.

Its function was simplicity itself. The elastic was slipped around the head at forehead level and positioned so that the pad hung down and covered the left ear. The weight on the pad ensured that the pad did not flap up in a high wind. One was then fully protected against damage to the hearing whilst running for a taxi or a bus. The dilemma when catching a taxi or a bus in a hurry is, of course, whether to stay put and wait for one to come along or whether, as is usual, to hurry towards one's destination, glancing over one's right shoulder every two steps to see whether one is being overtaken by the vehicle. The next thing one knows one is lying on the pavement, semi-deaf, having crashed one's left ear into a lamp-post or a tree. The wearer of a Muir Ear-Wig (as I amusingly called it) would be immune. It seems incredible to me that no manufacturer expressed the slightest interest in the device, probably because of professional jealousy, even when I added a Continental model to the range (this fitted the right ear – for when vehicles drove on the other side of the road).

The next invention was more complicated, consisting of a black box with dials, switches and an aerial, and a pair of trousers. In essence it was a radio-operated, remote-control zip fastener, a boon for any man who feels the call of nature at the wrong moment, such as a boxer who is about to be called into the ring and has his boxing-gloves on.

I rooted round in the suitcase and found several minor inventions which never got off the ground; a tiny net for collecting gold-fish bubbles to put into spirit-levels, a fine cambric moustache-snood for preventing the flotsam on the surface of minestrone soup from becoming entangled with the face hair, a silent alarm-clock for use at weekends, a rubber poker for prodding the artificial logs on electric fires . . .

I became aware of a rising mood of excitement, a feeling of expectancy. There had been one invention . . . what was it? . . . which I knew from the start was a winner. I thought hard. Of course! The Muir Patent All-Purpose Permanently Magnetised Wire! A seemingly ordinary coil of wire but, with its magnetic properties, capable of a thousand uses. Bent to the right shape it would pick up that nut which dropped off and fell into the engine of the car. Twisted straight it could be used to retrieve the house keys from behind the refrigerator. Sawn into little lengths and bent with pliers it would make a thousand magnetised staples. A piece balanced on the forefinger would point north . . .

But where was the wire? I bent over the suitcase but all I could see was a rusty old electric fan with lengths of rubber tubing and a packet of candles. What was *that* for? Ah, yes. Another brilliant idea which got nowhere. It was a device for bringing relief to dinner guests after one of my wife's curries.

You know how it is after a hot curry. Sweat breaks out on the forehead but the back of the neck goes cold and damp. My invention was designed to restore the back of the neck to its normal temperature by means of a controllable current of warm air. The fan would be connected to a socket, a row of candles would be lit and stood in front of the fan-blades and the lengths of rubber-tubing would be fixed to a small gantry in front of the candle-flames and unrolled, the ends being handed to each of the curry-eating guests. When the fan was switched on the guests would point their rubber tubes at the backs of their necks and the hot air would do its work. If by any chance the curry worked the other way round and heated the back of the neck whilst the forehead went cold and clammy then the guest could direct his flexible hose towards his forehead. It was a foolproof system. But it had gone very rusty over the years.

I carefully picked the fan and all the other bits out of the suitcase and peered in. Yes, there was the coil of Muir Patent All-Purpose Permanently Magnetised Wire all right. But ruined. The rust from the fan had oxidised the wire, which was little more than a small pile of brown dust.

I was holding the small pile of brown dust in my hand, a tear of regret for lost hopes meandering down my cheek, when my wife opened the cupboard door.

"What's that mess you're holding?" she asked curiously.

"The end of a dream," I said.

"Yes, but what *is* it?"

Sadly, and slowly, I gave answer:

"Wire my curry-fan has rusted."

WITH another Christmas at our throats in a mere ten days, the problem I confront is one that's been cropping up more and more these past few years. I've found out what I'm going to be given – and I don't want it.

I mention this predicament because I believe that somewhere within it lies the answer to the frequently asked question, 'What's gone wrong with the English Christmas?' To my mind, the deterioration dates back to whenever it was that people stopped buying each other presents and began buying each other gifts.

Because there is a very real difference. A present is something given in the hope that it will fulfil a need or expectation. Gifts are things you buy from Gift Shops.

No High Street today is complete without its Gift Shop, usually standing where late there was a small bakery, or a cobblers (how *did* the word for those eminently valuable tradesmen decline into its present expletive application?), or an ironmongers where you could get a key cut while you waited, or a fruiterer who stayed open till midnight, or a drapers where the old lady would cash a cheque for you. A Gift Shop is staffed by a man who wears a brown pseud jacket and puts the word 'only' in front of every price ('Only £386'). Its heavily tarted-up front-window displays a small figurine of a shepherdess with a clock in her navel, magnetised backgammon boards, Morrocan drink-trays that have nothing to lift them up by, and things known as Executive Toys; these are designed to sit on a broad expanse of empty desk and either hit one part of themselves against another part, or flash a succession of tiny lights in so random a fashion that you begin to realise why so many stockbrokers are jumping out of windows.

Those are gifts, as distinct from presents. They are the new 'giving-objects', artefacts designed not for use or enjoyment but simply as currency for Christmas transactions. Within the shop's bedizened interior you can purchase loo-seats that shine in the dark, Mickey Mouse sundials, cans of spray-on dandruff, battery-operated tooth-picks, polythene snowmen and a frozen mushroom-pizza with 'Happy Xmas' spelt out in anchovies.

And, of all these non-felt wants, the one that makes my heart sink almost to knee-level is the gift for which, so I've discovered, my well-meaning sister paid out her good money this Yuletide – a Scandinavian Candle-Making Kit. The cinema in my skull is already screening its presentation ceremony: "Oh, it's a candle-making kit! . . . And *Scandinavian*!"

"You sure you haven't got one?"

"I'm practically certain."

Are you familiar with that particular kind of jaw-muscle ache that comes only from maintaining a grateful smile for six hours? The kind where you become convinced you're going to have to send for a doctor because your face has locked? I'll be down with it practically all Christmas Day. And I can also tell you the moment I fear most.

"Aren't you going to try it? Oh, go on. Make a candle for Auntie Rose."

My handedness at all manual endeavours is so invincibly cack, I can hardly bear thinking about all those lumps of wax and rolls of wick and plastic moulds – and *hot tallow*!

If any of you are curious to know which seasonal tune I'll be carolling Christmas Day after the relatives have departed, I can already hum it for you:

'I'm cleaning off a white grease mess.'

The more haste the less speed

Proverb

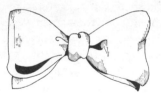

WHEN I was but a lad of some twelve sum-
mers (we only had summers when I was a lad) I was quiet and
introspective, much given to leaning against the bandstand on the
seafront at Broadstairs and undoing knots in string.

During one of my leans, when I was trying to perfect a technique of whistling 'Won't You Do, Do, Do What You Done, Done,
Done Before, Baby' whilst at the same time undoing a knot in a
piece of string, a disturbing thought struck me. I had made no
plans for the future. I had formulated absolutely no ambitions
whatever. And unless I came up with a few thoughts fairly quickly
I would suddenly wake up to find myself aged forty-eight and still
leaning up against the bandstand undoing knots in string.

Boys, unless they are the sons of clergymen, doctors or soldiers
in which case they know from the age of two that they are either
going to follow in father's footsteps or would rather drop dead than
so do, rarely have firm ideas on what they want to do with their
lives. The best most boys can rake up in the way of ambitions is to
own a 1,000,000 cc. Japanese motorbike that will do 250 mph, or
to have all their teeth pulled out so that they won't have to brush
them any more, or to marry Raquel Welch. Only a few can hope to
achieve any of these.

I proved to have been made of more thoughtful clay. After a
mere eight leans I came up with not one ambition but *three*.

My three ambitions could be classified as (*a*) achieving a triumph
of physical skill, (*b*) proving to myself that I possessed courage and
initiative and (*c*) aiming high in the matter of a career.

More specifically these ambitions consisted of (*a*) managing to

22

touch the tip of my nose with my tongue, (*b*) cycling at full speed along Broadstairs jetty with my eyes shut and completing eight turns of the pedals without opening them, and (*c*) becoming a recognised expert at something.

Alas, it seems that the loftier one raises the structure of one's aspirations the more likely – life being what it is – that it will descend about one's ears like cheap hair cream on a hot day.

After months of constant practice in school, at church, on buses, I finally had to admit to myself that there was an unbridgeable gap twixt the end of my tongue and the tip of my nose and never the twain were going to meet. The trouble was that I had an extra-long upper lip, as normally found on horses, so I decided I would be better employed on obscuring this by growing a moustache. I concentrated hard on forcing the moustache out and my single-mindedness worked – eight years later it emerged. I have it still.

My failure to cycle along the jetty with my eyes closed for eight turns of the pedals was a great disappointment to me at the time. But looking back I take great comfort in the fact that although it was high tide and the light was none too good on that cold February afternoon and there was a strong crosswind I did not lose my nerve and open my eyes. It was just that after six turns of the pedals I ran out of jetty.

My ambition to become recognised as an expert in something was, I admit, a little on the vague side. I took it for granted that it would be in some esoteric area like ferret-sexing, or comparative religion but I held no strong views on which; I just wanted to be an expert. Well, it has happened. A paltry forty-six years later my ambition has been fulfilled. It is fairly well recognised now by most civilised nations that I am the acknowledged expert on The Maintenance of Carpets in Households which include an Incontinent Afghan Hound Puppy.

My pre-eminence in the subject became undisputed when I began to write books for children about an Afghan puppy called What-a-mess. These were so successful, the sales soaring to double figures within months of publication, that hardly a week passes now without a postcard flooding in asking my advice in the matter of carpets and puppies. As postage rates are rising so high that it will soon be cheaper to send a letter by taxi this seems to be the moment to put into print my own experience of the puppy versus carpet problem and how I cope with it.

What-a-mess in the books is a fictional puppy based on our own small Afghan. He is a normal little chap, as well-behaved as any Afghan puppy. That is to say, he steals all food that is not under lock and key, chews chair legs, sits on top of the hedge and breaks it, jumps over the fence and disappears and digs holes four-feet deep in the lawn. Afghans are natural diggers. You will find no record of an Afghan Hound ever having been incarcerated in Colditz for the simple reason that no Kommandant could keep an Afghan in Colditz long enough to get its name and Kennel-Club number. I would give a fairly lazy Afghan eight minutes to dig its way out of Colditz. Ten if it was solid rock beneath.

And ours is as intelligent as any Afghan puppy. He knows perfectly well the difference between outdoors and indoors; he knows that in one he can streak about at full speed, dig and answer the calls of nature in peace and seclusion and in the other he can sleep. The trouble is that he gets them the wrong way round. He sleeps outside then comes into the house, tries to dig a hole in the parquet floor, leaps on to the dining-room table and sits in the mashed potatoes, gets up a speed of forty knots along the upstairs landing and then, when your back is turned, leaves a 9" × 5" damp map of Corsica sinking slowly into the pile of the carpet.

Further, once the 9" × 5" map of Corsica has been bestowed upon the carpet, the puppy has a compulsion to keep it fresh. To replenish it hourly. And then, to be on the safe side, to start a little reserve Sardinia by the radiator.

It was only by diligent observation and careful reasoning that I was able to make the breakthrough, to beat the Corsica problem and establish my reputation as the world's leading expert on the matter.

We have our Mrs Hayes who comes in twice a week and goes through the house like a tornado, elbows going like pistons, carrying all dirt and dust before her and leaving furniture and carpets like new. Mrs Hayes went away for three months to visit her son in Australia and I noticed that the maps of Corsica on the carpet increased ten-fold in her absence. I pondered why. Then I had a flash of inspiration. Dogs instinctively return to the scene of their crime. It's a matter of scent, or something, but the presence of a damp map of Corsica prompts the beast to re-anoint the same patch of carpet. Answer? Scrub out all traces of the first map of Corsica and the puppy is not tempted.

And so it proved. Mrs Hayes returned from Australia, went at the carpet with cleaner, brush and vacuum and the puppy soon lost interest.

From this experience I formulated a maxim which all carpet and Afghan puppy owners might well ponder. As far as *my* carpets are concerned:

The more Hayes'd the less peed.

Your money or your life!

Attr. Dick Turpin

IF people really do profit by their mistakes, by rights I should now be one of the richest men in the country. As just one example of what's happened to me in the rue-it-yourself area, let me tell you about the time I decided to avail myself of a Computer Dating Service.

Although that title may sound like a service for people desirous of dating a computer, it's actually a sort of electronic Match Factory. If you're a male, they give you a blue form on which you are asked to tick off your particular preferences and predilections in regard to the opposite sex. That form is then fed into an impressive machine which makes a whirring noise as it compares your blue form with a whole bunch of pink forms it has previously swallowed on behalf of various ladies who've signed on for the service. If the ticks on your blue one happen to coincide exactly with those on somebody's pink one, the ingenious mechanism utters the technological equivalent of 'snap!', ejects that pink one and there she is, the mate that fate had you created for.

What put me on to the service was hearing a chap in my office holding forth to an interested group about how he'd met his wife through Computer Dating. The reason he was going on with such fervour about it was that it had happened the previous day and they'd already been married eight years. So the point he was trying to impress on us was that although such accidents do occur, they only ever happen through pilot-error; in other words, careless or incorrect completion of the blue form.

So that became the part of the procedure over which I took the greatest pains. The first section of it, requesting my own personal history – all that 'where-were-you-born-and-what-did-you-do-before-that?' stuff – that presented no problems at all, unless you count having to ask the invigilator whether 'Freckles' ought to be written inside the box headed 'State any serious childhood ailments'.

It was when I came to Section Two, 'What type of opposite sex person are you seeking?', that I made myself stop and think hard. Mindful of the unhappy encounter resulting from my colleague's failure to supply adequate detail at this point, I set myself to writing what amounted to an in-depth profile of the woman my life had been spent in search of. So carefully did I outline the specifications for my ideal, so minutely did I describe the characteristics I'd always failed to find in a partner, my text over-ran the little boxes and I had to request four extra blue forms.

When they fed them into the machine it soon became obvious that no previous client had ever been this painstaking. Something inside the mechanism spluttered, the overhead lights dimmed, red bulbs blinked on and off and the sprinkler-system came on. "Please leave by the emergency exit," the machine's trainer said somewhat abruptly. "We'll have to send you your answer in the post." Sure enough, the letter arrived three days later, giving me a name, detailed arrangements for meeting under the clock at Waterloo Station and a description by which I would recognise her.

We had an unforgettable evening. It included a visit to 'Singa-longa-Max' where we even sunga-longa the intermission, a *table à deux* at the Curry House and an arm-in-arm stroll through the all-night Tesco's. It was there, in the Pickles And Spices aisle, that I said, "Your place or mine?"

When we entered her front door, she indicated that I should go on up while she put the chain on. When I entered the lounge, the first thing I saw was her husband.

"Hallo," he said. "Had a nice evening?"

"Yes thanks, Dad," I replied. He went up to bed, my mother put her apron on to make a cup of tea and I sat there brooding about computers and how they always take your requests so *literally*.

I didn't come to any real conclusions, except that although Computer Dating Services may be all right for some, if you're anything like me and the chap at the office all you're likely to end up with is what you might call Dick Turpin's choice:

Your mummy or your wife.

27

'Hello! Hello! Who's Your Lady Friend?'

Music Hall Song

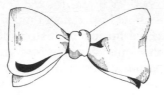

WE, the duly and democratically elected officers of the Thorpe Players Amateur Dramatic Society (tickets available at the door or from Nellie at the Thorpe Village Shop) are not easily panicked. We like to think, and audiences who miss the last bus home tend to agree with us, that we act slowly. We tend to weigh the pros and cons carefully before agreeing to do nothing rather than rush precipitously into action.

I refer you to the crisis of '63 (see the files of *Staines and Egham News* for full reportage) when, at the Annual General Meeting, a splinter group endeavoured to outvote the committee and accept the merger bid from the Egham Thespians. It was a nasty moment for us traditionalists. Egham Thespians had a reputation for going in for somewhat racier productions than was our wont; their staging of *Getting Gertie's Garter* caused many an Egham eyebrow to uplift, I can tell you. And the splinter group outnumbered us by five to four (it was an unusually high turnout for an AGM). But we did not panic. Just before the vote my vice-chairperson and prompter, Mrs Spink, rose to her feet and quietly reminded the meeting of the dramatic traditions which we had always cherished in the Players. After forty-five minutes of this I noticed that two of the splinter group – the old Dinwiddie brothers – were fast asleep so I quickly called a vote and we staved off the threat by four votes to three.

No, panic does not come easily to us fathers of Thorpe Players. But it came one black Thursday, just three days before the opening of our most ambitious production to date, a full musical comedy adapted by me from a work by Mr Sandy Wilson.

Most dramatic societies consist mainly of women and their problem is how to cast *The Importance of Being Earnest* with forty-two f's to select from but only two m's, the two m's consisting usually of a retired Civil Servant with an inaudible voice and no memory and an enthusiastic youth six feet seven in height with terminal acne. Our problem was the other way round – we had plenty of men but only one woman. This unusual circumstance came about when work began on the motorway near Thorpe and the village filled with sturdy, rather playful construction workers. For some reason the girls in our Society seemed to prefer their society to ours. The one lady we have, our leading and only lady, Miss Tozer, is so ample of build and homely of countenance that she has not as yet been offered temptation.

Finding it impossible to locate a play with a cast of 14 m:1 f I decided to adapt Mr Wilson's musical comedy *The Boy Friend*. I twisted the story round so that it was not about a party of schoolgirls but of schoolboys. They go on an outing to Guildford and all fall in love with an adorable little French au-pair girl Antoinette (Miss Tozer). The songs adapted quite well ('Sur la Plage' became 'On the Towpath', 'A Room in Bloomsbury' became 'A Tent at Penton Hook', etc.). The title had to be changed from *The Boy Friend*, of course. I originally considered calling it *The Girl Friend* but I eventually decided on *The Lady Friend* as being more suitable for our audiences, some of whom come from Virginia Water and the superior end of Egham Hythe.

Rehearsals seemed to go swimmingly. Miss Tozer's frame may have been vast but, as so often is the case with enormous ladies, her voice was a high, light soprano and she was in fine condition. Mr Haddock, the organist, managed to repair the bellows of the harmonium with a bicycle puncture outfit and the musical accompaniment was strong and rich. We gaily bought a new bulb for our footlight.

Then, on the Thursday before our opening on the Monday, Mr Haddock turned up at my house, his face a mask of woe.

"Out with it, Haddock," I said instantly. "What has happened, man?"

Mutely he swung on his heel. I followed him out of the gate and along Coldharbour Lane towards our theatre, Thorpe Village Hall (originally a medieval tithe barn. Good brickwork but not as interesting as the church which is partly Saxon with fine modern stained glass windows). Entering the hall he flung out an arm and pointed towards where, below the stage, stood the harmonium.

"Great Heavens!" I breathed. The right-hand side of the keyboard had disappeared. From Middle C leftwards all was well but above Middle C there was nothing. It was horrible, horrible. Like the grin of somebody who has had half his teeth removed. I was looking at a harmonium capable of accompanying bass singers and light baritones but not tenors or sopranos.

"And we open Monday," he said with a terrible calmness. "Who could have *done* this? Why? Why?" I comforted him as best I could.

"We of the governing body of the Thorpe Players do not yield easily to panic," I said. "It is clear that we must replace Miss Tozer with a lady baritone, and pretty damn' chop-chop. Let us to work."

Thorpe village ladies turned out to be a nest of singing birds. All of them sopranos. Few of them could get as low as Middle C, let alone sing 'I Could Be Happy With You' completely below it. Mrs Hayes made a valiant effort but only succeeded in bursting a – mercifully non-essential – button on her blouse.

Like most police work it demanded dogged patience and the skin of a rhinoceros. Late Friday afternoon I found myself addressing our last hope of finding a baritone leading lady, Mrs Knight of the fishshop.

"Nora," I said thickly, my eyes red with fatigue, "I need a special type of woman on Monday night. How low can you get?"

Looking back on it I am only glad that the fishshop was in Virginia Water and I was slapped on the face with a side of smoked salmon rather than a kipper.

It was a morose organist indeed who accompanied me on a sad stroll through the village on Saturday morning, all hope seemingly lost. "Are all Thorpe voices high?" I queried petulantly. "Are there no low? Is there not *one* low?"

At that moment we hove in sight of the allotments, those patches of ground on which a gracious Urban District Council allows grateful ratepayers to grow leeks and potatoes and so forth at a nominal rental.

"Look!" shouted Mr Haddock suddenly, grabbing my arm and then breaking for the first time since I had known him into swear words, "Great Handel, our most illustrious immigrant!" Following

Between the devil and the deep blue sea

Proverbial saying

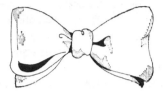

HOW splendid and Faust-like to be given the choice of yielding to Beelzebub or diving into the briny. And how seldom life offers up such dramatic alternatives. In most people's lives, i.e. mine, the hinges which determine one's destiny are hidden and the only decisions which one is given the chance to make are on a lesser scale, usually in the area of choosing between navel oranges at 10p each or a smaller, knobblier variety at 6p, or between the hard-wearing herring-bone tweed suit and the trendy beige.

But sometimes life gives a hiccough and presents one with a dilemma which is both dramatic and difficult to resolve.

My life, to date, has not been the stuff of which heroic auto-biographies are made. Indeed it has been extremely difficult to whip up a paragraph calculated to get the turnstiles humming at the prospect of hearing me speak to the Thorpe Derby And Joan Club. Not for me those author's blurbs along the lines of: 'After leaving Eton under a cloud he served for some time in the Foreign Legion before escaping and helping to found a trout-farm in Chile. A spell as a lumberjack in Cheltenham was followed by being elected a fellow of All Souls from which he progressed to becoming the guttering-buyer of a departmental store in Atlanta, Georgia . . .' etc. My progress has been more like a Poohstick's, carried along by a sluggish current from one patch of weeds to another.

And yet it happened. The Big Decision.

The four most emotionally satisfying events of my pale life have been (*a*) marrying, (*b*) buying my first boat, (*c*) getting rid of the boat, (*d*) being elected Rector of the University of St

35

Andrews, Fife, Scotland. And it is the last of these of which I speak.

Rectorship is not only a peculiarly Scottish institution, it is also just plain peculiar. The Rector is elected solely by the students and his loyalty is entirely to the students and their welfare, yet by virtue of the high standing of his office he chairs the University Court, which meets once a month.

My first year in office was wholly delightful. I flew up to Edinburgh on British Airways Shuttle Service – an admirable service once you have swallowed the unpalatable fact that when the trolley comes up the gangway it is only to take your ticket: there are no drinks. Which is rather like realising at an accident that there is no hot, sweet tea. There were a couple of other slight complications that had to be got used to, e.g. on the drive from the airport to St Andrews the toll bridge does not take luncheon vouchers. And on the Motorway there is no Exit 7. As the route to St Andrews requires you to come off at Exit 8 this means that you overshoot and hurtle towards Perth unless you are vigilant. Why the Exits go from 6 to 8 seems to be a mystery locked in the bosom of the Kingdom of Fife.

Once in St Andrews I unpack in room fifteen of the Star Hotel. This is bang in the middle of this wholly delightful grey granite fishing village and room fifteen has advantages; it is, perhaps, two yards away from the church bell which tolls the hours, but it is large and warm.

One of the problems with paying a monthly visit to the east coast of Scotland is anticipating the weather. One leaves the decadent south-east of England in the hard-wearing herring-bone tweed and is projected into another clime. St Andrews, it seems to me, gets the best of whatever weather is hanging about Scotland, but this is somewhat unpredictable. So, with the connivance of the management of the hotel, I leave two garments in their broom-cupboard so that I will not be caught unprepared. For an onslaught of cold weather I have left a duffel coat; a vast, fawn tent which did service during the last war on the bridges of many of His Majesty's vessels, going down twice, and which has since served as a lying-in bed for the Afghan Hound to have her puppies on, a comforter for motor-car engines in frosty weather and a surrogate womb for seed potatoes. Should I run into a heat wave I have left a T-shirt. This cost me 15p at an auction in aid of a book-trade

36

charity. It is a deeply unpleasant shade of bright blue and has across its front the words, 'Proof-readers Rule, O.J.?'

Members of the University Court were most kind to their ignorant and amateur chairman. Professors, lecturers, local council members and other Court participants leaned over backwards to put their chairman at ease and I was not at all worried until about the seventh meeting. Then I was aware of something rather strange. When I arrived for the meeting at 10 a.m. the whole assemblage was there as though to welcome me but although one face was glum the rest were smiling. As other meetings followed I became more aware of the pattern. At one meeting the University Architect would be downcast and the rest happy. A month later the Quaestor and Factor would look extremely miserable and the rest smiling.

The University, arguably the best university in the world, has a most efficient grapevine. What I learned from the grapevine was rather surprising. Apparently I had always turned up at the Court meeting wearing the hard-wearing herring-bone tweed. Members of the Court, racked with ennui after an hour of their chairman, had begun a sweepstake as to when I would turn up dressed differently. Hence the one unhappy face who had drawn that month only to see me turn up in the same old herring-bone tweed.

The grapevine also revealed that this month the one who stood to gain from my change of clothing was the University Secretary, David Devine. The sweepstake suddenly took on a new significance. It is Mr Devine who passes my claims for expenses and I am rather keen on upping my drive from Edinburgh airport to St Andrews from a bicycle to a moped. If I can cause him to win the sweepstake – which stands, the grapevine tells me, at a jackpot of 95p – I stand every chance of having my higher expenses passed by Devine intervention.

I swung into action immediately. I have a small wardrobe, and an even smaller collection of clothes within it. But I bundled the lot into a plastic bag for taking to the dry cleaners so that I would have a selection of clothes with which to win Mr Devine his jackpot. It is a curious thing about laundries and dry-cleaners that once one has packed the stuff up to be taken one somehow assumes that the job is done and one forgets all about it. Suffice it to say that yesterday I suddenly found the plastic bag with all my clothes scrunched up in it and tomorrow I am off to St Andrews. Our local 24-Hour Cleaners are swifter than most but even they take three days.

I resolved to dry-clean the suits myself. All one needs, I reasoned, is a bucket of French chalk, a gallon of carbon tetrachloride and something to tumble the mixture and the clothes around in.

I found my something just along the road where they are building an extension to our local motorway – a nearly new, clean, bright cement-mixer. I tipped the bag of clothes in, poured in the fluid and the powder, started the motor and stood back to watch as the engine roared away and the drum spun merrily round. All was going well until I noticed, to my horror, a huge, revolving lorry backing remorselessly towards my mixer. I shouted out but all the machinery was making a shocking noise. As I watched helplessly the revolving bit of the lorry slowly tilted and about half a ton of wet cement poured into my mixer. My entire wardrobe is now half a yard of the M.25 (Sunbury to Basingstoke extension).

So if I am to wear something different tomorrow I will have to face the University Court wearing one of the two garments hanging up in the Star Hotel's broom cupboard. My choice is pathetically simple:

Between the duffel and the cheap, blue 'T'.

'Oh, Mr Porter, What Shall I Do?'

Music Hall Song

I had a profound and disturbing thought recently – not that I don't have them quite often, of course – but this one really brought me down. I was suddenly struck by the fact that, despite the many years I've been on the entertainment scene, nobody has ever tried to bribe or corrupt me.

I can't tell you how *small* that made me feel. I mean, every newspaper you pick up nowadays seems to have a story about somebody in the show-business receiving illicit offers of call-girls or Greek villas or Swiss bank-deposits. But me – never. Nothing. Not even a book-token.

The more I thought about that, the lower my spirits sank. To such an extent that the very next day I went round to my agent and put it to him straight. "Are there any jobs going where a chap can get himself tarnished?"

He's a nice fellow, my agent, very good-hearted, a warm and wonderful friend, but anything that's the least bit out-of-the-way you have to explain it as to a sleepy child. "What I would like you to find me," I said, enunciating very slowly and with plenty of pauses so it would sink in, "is a post of trust . . . which I can betray . . . for gain."

A small cloud of incomprehension settled about his face. "A position of power," I went on doggedly, "that I can abuse. For my own contemptible purposes. And when I say contemptible –"

"Before you go into that, Den," he broke in, "I had something come up I meant to ring you about. Some holiday camp. They're enquiring for somebody from the wireless to judge a Beauty Contest. The money's not much but you get a cooked supper and . . ."

But I was no longer listening. It was perfect! Little though he realised it, corruption-wise it could not have suited my purpose better. Well, we've all read about what goes on at those Beauty Contests, haven't we? all Those squalid behind-the-scenes episodes, where a desperate group of beautiful girls, all seeking the coveted First Prize, vie with each other to win the attention of a judge? Swiftly my mind ran through the scenario. "Really, Miss Orkneys And Shetlands, are you hinting that I should show you special favour? If that is so, we'd better sit down and discuss it. Tell me, child, are you not a little too warm in that sash . . .?"

Out loud, I said, "Book me on the next train."

Well, it wasn't what you'd call a large holiday camp. It wasn't even what you'd call a medium-size holiday camp. What you would call it, I think, was a dump. It had previously been an open prison, I was told, but the present owner – a certain Miss Dora Tapwater – had managed to convert it to holiday camp standards by sealing up a few more entrances and adding extra barbed wire. For what I had in mind, though, it could not have been more suitable. So, immediately on arrival, I presented Miss Tapwater with the text of an announcement to be put out over her loud-speaker system: 'The judge for the Beauty Contest is now available for consultation in Chalet Number Two.'

"You're not up to any funny business, are you?" she asked sharply. "Because I'm not running that kind of holiday camp here. This place is for parents and families, so I don't allow goings-on."

Throttling back the impulse to enquire how she thought parents managed to achieve families without resort to goings-on, I put on my most guileless face and assured her I was merely seeking background detail from the girls. Although remaining suspicious – "I scan every chalet door through a marine telescope after Lights Out!" – she finally consented to my veiled invitation being broadcast.

I had to sit in Chalet Two for nigh on three hours before I got a nibble. Then, just as my scented cachous were beginning to wear off, an envelope was pushed under my door. Leaping to my feet, I ripped it open and pulled out a sheet of perfumed notepaper and a photograph. I scanned the note first. 'Dear Judge, I would do anything to win First Prize.' The word 'anything' was underlined. Three times. In red! Pulses pounding, I read on. 'Soon as that old cow with the telescope nods off, I'll be back with an open

40

mind and two bottles of milk stout. P.S. Hope the photo don't shock you. It shows me in the costume I wore when I won this same contest last year.'

As it happens, I didn't even get as far as looking at what she was wearing. When I turned to the photograph, the first thing that leapt to my eyes was the inscription on the trophy she was holding.

What I'd forgotten about holiday camps, you see, was that when they say they cater to every member of the family, they really do mean every member. Across the trophy, in bold capitals, were the triumphant words: 'First Prize, Most Glamorous Granny Contest.'

Thirty seconds after the words had sunk in, the camp's proprietor had her lonely vigil interrupted by an urgent telephone call. The message, in as disguised a voice as its still uncorrupted owner could muster, must have sounded like the echo of an old song:

Oh, Miss Tapwater, Watch Chalet Two.

If you have tears, prepare to shed them now

Shakespeare
Julius Caesar, Act III, Sc. 2

IT seems that in meteorological offices all over the country the sea-weed has been dying in handfuls and not a corn has throbbed on a meteorological toe for months. The chaps held a meeting about it and issued an alarming statement. They say that the weather pattern is changing and we are due for a run of very hot summers.

This is bad news of the worst sort. If they had forecast a run of cold winters there would be no cause for dismay. As a nation we know how to cope with cold winters: at the first light fall of snow paraffin disappears off the market, the miners go on strike, all railway-line points freeze solid and doctors warn that Algerian 'flu is about to sweep the country and decimate the population. We just grit our teeth, force a smile and suffer on.

But hot summers are another dish of tea entirely. Look what happened when we had a bit of sun in the summer of '76; reservoirs dried to a puddle, lawns went brown, roads melted and doctors warned that Yugoslavian 'flu was about to sweep the country and slay one in eight. We all went about panting like retrievers, wearing too many clothes and longing for a cold bath which we couldn't have because there wasn't enough water.

It seems to me that if hot summers are going to be our lot from now on then we should prepare for them. Make a few plans.

Take clothes. I have given the matter some thought and it seems to me that we British are not going to go mad and dress like Hawaiian beachboys whatever the temperature. We will continue to wear our suits to work, perhaps leaving off our waistcoats when the thermometer rises above 100°F. So what we must do is provide

42

our clothes with suitable ventilation.

Go to your nearest ironmonger and buy yourself what is called a leather punch. This is like a pair of pliers with a spiky thing on the end of one of the jaws. This spiky thing is really a collection of long holes of different widths. Select the widest hole, which is about a third of an inch, and systematically work your way over your suit, punching holes through the fabric at the rate of twelve to the foot. When you have completely perforated the suit do the same to your underwear.

Now you might think that all these holes in both your suit and your underwear will result in loss of modesty. Not so. Whilst wearing your ventilated clothes you keep gently on the move at all times, even when sitting down. Just a slight movement – a gentle shimmy as though moved by distant Latin American music – is enough to prevent the holes in underclothing and outer clothing from coinciding.

Keeping the home cool is a more complicated problem. An ideal method is to open the front door and the back door and to get an elephant to stand at the back door flapping its ears. This results in a pleasing through-draught.

Another procedure which gives good results is to save up odds and ends of household fluids like the washing-up water, unconsumed tea or milk which has gone sour, and fling the lot over the drawing-room wallpaper. This is known as 'cooling by evaporation'.

Getting to sleep at night can be a problem. One solution is to fling open the bedroom window, chuck a pillow out, follow it and sleep outside on the lawn.

A better method is to put your pyjamas into the refrigerator for an hour before retiring. Don't put them in the deep-freeze or severe lacerations can result.

Cars are a frightful problem during periods of heat. For one thing they tend to boil over if you stop at a traffic-light for more than four seconds. This is because of the anti-freeze in the radiator. Anti-freeze is a mixture of alcohol and water which has the property of not freezing in cold weather but, unhappily, boiling at the drop of a hat in hot weather. What you must do is to drain off the anti-freeze and refill the radiator with a mixture which is almost all water with hardly any alcohol in it at all. So park the car outside a pub, run a hose in from the radiator and ask the barman to fill her up with British keg bitter, the alcohol content of which is negligible.

Always carry a siphon of soda-water in the boot. When a car has been standing a few minutes in the sun you can fry eggs on the plastic upholstery. Before entering the car spray the seats generously with soda-water to cool them, then take your shirt off and mop the seats thoroughly. Put shirt back on (see above: 'cooling by evaporation').

The most grievous problem of all with cars is stopping the tyres from exploding. Air expands when warm and on a hot day in the South of France you can hear tyres popping off all around you like artillery fire.

The only hope is to keep the sun off the tyres as much as possible. A good idea is to hire a furniture van, get your wife to precede you along the road and when you need to park just drive up the ramp and into the back of the van. But this is rather too expensive for most people and there is a snag – the tyres of the van tend to explode.

The French sometimes drape little raffia mats over their tyres when parking in the sun but these mats blow off or slide down unless nailed firmly to the tyres – a stratagem which I found to be self-defeating.

The tyre problem seemed insoluble until I put my mind to it and came up with a complete answer. Here is what you do. Take a train or a plane to Edinburgh. Half-way up Princes Street there is a shop which sells tartans and knitting patterns. Buy a knitting pattern for a highland bonnet and half a hundredweight of knitting wool the same colour as your car.

When you get home take the knitting pattern and multiply all the numbers of stitches by ten. Start knitting. When you have finished you will have a giant highland bonnet. Knit another three giant highland bonnets. Carry them out to the car, jack up each wheel in turn and fit it with a bonnet, making sure that the rim of the bonnet fits snugly round the tread and the pom-pom is dead centre. Your tyres will now be permanently shaded from the sun for as long as you care to leave the car parked. To drive away simply jack the wheels up again and remove the bonnets.

To work! Don't let the next hot summer catch you unawares.

If you have tyres, prepare to shade them *now*.

Falstaff will die of a sweat

Shakespeare
King Henry V, Part 2, Epilogue

"I F you maintain your garden regularly," said the voice on the radio, "you can have something fresh-cut every day." I reached for my note-book. "The only something fresh-cut my garden gives me every day," I wrote, "is lawn-mower lead."

It was yet another telling point in the long list of indictments I was preparing against my garden lawn. My case against it, indeed against the whole institution of suburban back-lawns, had begun earlier that summer when, aching back bent over purpling knees, I suddenly let fall my copy of *Weeders Digest* and thought, "Something about all this is basically *unsound*. There's Nature growing weeds twenty-four hours a day and here's me pulling them out two hours a week."

That's when I started compiling my '*j'accuse*' notebook. Its next entry was a detailed breakdown of the iniquitous price of grass seed; plus, of course, the additional items required for nourishing it – mulch, fertiliser, nutrients and the like. Totting those up, I soon realised that my lawn was more expensively dressed than my children.

More pampered, too. One fertiliser on the list demanded to be applied every six hours. I defy anyone to find me a human activity more demeaning than getting up in the middle of the night to give a patch of grass its 2 a.m. feed.

What also has to be taken into account in estimating the financial burden of a lawn are the various decorative items you place upon it: things like gnomes, small windmills, bird-baths. Any one of those can cost enough to wipe you out in the bad times. For a small grey bird-bath, the chap in my Garden Suppliers was asking no

45

less than £37! "You've gone beyond the limits of credibility," I told him. "Not even St Francis would pay £37 for a bird-bath."

And after you've spent all that money, what are you actually left with? In my case, despite all the outlay and the effort and the bending over it and the trudging up and down it, that lawn still looked like it was written by Samuel Beckett. If you gazed down upon it from the bedroom window, its surface resembled nothing so much as one of those old-fashioned water biscuits, the kind that had little brown humps sticking up all over. The only time my grass could offer an onlooker the slightest vestige of aesthetic pleasure was when it was under three inches of snow.

The case the notebook finally presented was so unanswerable I took the only sensible course. Over the following weekend I had the whole lawn removed and a plastic one laid down.

Even at this distance, I can hear your gasps of revulsion. But bear with me. There is much to be said in favour of a plastic lawn. 'Synthetic turf' it's called – American, of course – and it comes in rolls. The one great thing about it, though, is that when you lay it down, it *stays* there – no brown humps, no weeds and no pathetic gasps for mulch or nutriment.

I'd go further. A summer evening offers few pleasures sweeter than settling back in a deck-chair on your synthetic turf and listening contentedly to the man next door giving himself a coronary pushing his heavy mower. For that's another count against natural grass that I neglected to mention. They that live by the sward shall perish by the sward.

Mind you, I don't want to give the impression that the plastic version is completely free of drawbacks. It does possess one minor disadvantage – if it gets the slightest bit wet, it rots. However, all that amounts to in practical terms is that whenever there's a threat of rain, you just have to be careful to go outside, roll the lengths of turf up again, bring them all indoors and lean them against the walls of your dining room till the sun returns. A small price to pay I call it, especially as it also guarantees you'll hardly ever be able to invite people to dinner any more.

So it's a lifetime of ease and indolence that I'm now offering lawn-lovers. And all you have to do in return is bear in mind that one little warning which Shakespeare so presciently anticipated:

False turf will die if it's wet.

46

And thereby hangs a tale

Shakespeare

As You Like It, Act II, Sc. 7

THE fact has to be admitted that I am to nature what Dame Margot Fonteyn is to non-ferrous sheet-metal welding. I know which end is which of Afghan hounds and Burmese cats, I can tell the difference between a daffodil and a horse, I can mow the lawn if the machine starts first time but beyond these I am as a child. Worse than a child, really, because most children, particularly girls, seem to know everything about animals from birth.

It was this lack of empathy with feathered and furry things which led to the tragic happening which occurred to the lamb Angus on the morning of Saturday, 10th April.

What I was doing half-way up a Highland mountain on a chilly April day can be explained in a trice. I was convalescing after a bout of virus pneumonia. Why I accepted that invitation from my friend who raised sheep on a hill-farm near Fort William rather than spend the time lolling on some warm beach in the sun is evidence that pneumonia weakens the brain as well as the body. It certainly weakens the body. For weeks after leaving hospital I had to use both hands to lift a potato crisp.

It was in this weak and emaciated state that I journeyed to Scotland. The train journey by sleeper was a nightmare. When I had finished playing with all the little folding shelves in the sleeper compartment and had worked out what the bit of bent wire by the door was for (it is for holding the door ajar) and what was the purpose of the hook with the bit of chamois leather beneath it (it is for a gentleman to hang his pocket watch upon) and had taken a sip from the carafe of pond water and unrolled the paper drugget and tried the taps and switched the lighting to 'dim', I found that I had not enough strength to pull the bedclothes apart and get into the bunk and had, perforce, to wrap myself in the spare blanket and sleep on top of it.

The rhythmic 'ga-dunk, ga-dunk, ga-dunk' of iron wheels upon railway track had a pleasantly soothing effect and the emaciated body soon yielded itself to sleep. But not for long at any one stretch. The overnight train to Fort William stopped eighteen times en route, each time with a jerk which sent the emaciated body rolling off the bunk and onto the floor.

It was a hollow-eyed, pale travesty of a guest who presented himself at the hill farm in Ardgour, anxious to be no trouble and slip easily into the sheep-tending routine.

It was not easy. For one thing, my dear friend and host was an ex-Captain in the Navy, used to giving instructions briefly, crisply and once only. And hill-farming seems to have a vocabulary all its own. I never once understood a blind word I was told ('Up the scarp to the bothy . . . count the tups there . . . then go gathering . . .'). For another thing, life on a sheep farm is physical and I had hardly any physique left.

My first job was fairly harmless. It was to clear boulders from a meadow. This is a simple form of drudgery which was historically performed by convicts until Miss Fry or Mr Howard persuaded the government that it was utterly inhuman and convicts should be given more rewarding tasks like picking oakum or running up a treadmill.

I squelched through the mud in my wellies and found the meadow, which was pock-marked with huge stones. I bent down and lifted a smallish specimen, managing to feel chill and break out in a sweat at the same time with the effort. As I stood there cradling the stone I was overwhelmed with a feeling that I was diminishing, as indeed I was; I was steadily sinking into the mud. When I had sunk to waist level my feet touched bedrock and I sank no more. Two hours later the tractor pulled me out – with the sound of a hippopotamus kissing its mate – and my host decided to put me onto lighter duties; getting the lambs into the Land-Rover trailer for taking to their new feeding pasture by the loch.

I staggered up a hill with Raymond, the shepherd, to sort out the beasts – we had to separate the ewes from the non-ewes – and urge them downhill towards the trailer. The trailer was rather cunningly adapted for this job, having a kind of platform which enabled two layers of sheep to be transported. Raymond grabbed the lambs by their wool and stuffed them into the lower compartment. He managed to get sixteen of them in and they stood placidly facing forward. He swung up the baseboard and locked them in.

"There's one left," he said. "It's Angus – always a wee bitty playful is Angus. You put him in the top compartment while I go and fetch the Land-Rover."

He left. I looked round and there was Angus right behind me, eyes innocent, baa-ing gently.

"Get in, Angus!" I said, without much hope. He gazed at me placidly. "If you take a running jump you'll make it," I pleaded. "Up, boy!" I coaxed.

I took hold of his wool and tried to lift him. A red mist swam before my eyes and the trembling began again. I tried running round him, barking like a sheepdog. He looked at me and went 'baa' vaguely. How on earth was I to get a sturdily built lamb onto that upper part of the trailer, some four feet off the ground?

I sat down in the mud and thought it over. Lifting was out of the question in my state of health. An inclined plane?

Into the house I rushed. There was an old Victorian sofa in the drawing room. In a flash I had whipped off its four casters. Up to the bathroom for a tin of sticking-plasters and then out to the workshop for an eight-foot plank.

Angus took it all very well, I must say. He stood perfectly still while I taped the castars to his feet. I propped the plank against the platform in the back of the trailer and coaxed Angus to walk forward until he was standing on the bottom of it. Then gently, oh so gently, I wheeled Angus up the plank and into the trailer. I had done it! I whipped the plank away and was about to slam down the top half of the trailer door when I heard a trundling noise.

Horror! The trailer was not on level ground. It was pointing slightly uphill and Angus was rolling backwards towards the open door.

I sprang forwards and managed to get my hands on his bottom before he rolled out and fell to the ground. I gave him a strong push as an experiment. He trundled forward until his nose was against the forward compartment and then began to roll back, accelerating as he went. I stopped him again and calculated that I would just

49

have time to slam the hatch down on him if I gave him a good, strong push.

I pushed and reached up for the top of the door. But something went wrong. The top half of the door was held up by a catch and it took me that fatal second to disconnect the catch and slam down the door. In that second Angus had rolled back and – even now I find it painful to even think about it – his little tail was trapped in the door and severed.

Small wonder that I have slept but fitfully since then. The thought of little Angus living out his life rudderless, imperfect, an object of scorn and mockery to his fellow lambs has haunted me. But what could I do? Nothing, I told myself. Tailless he must remain.

But yesterday I was driving back from visiting a friend in the West Country when, out of the corner of my eye, I saw a sign in a shop-window. I failed to register what sort of shop it was, a butcher's or a bookshop I fancy, but the sign said 'For Sale, Cheap. Lambs Tails. From Shakespeare'. (I take that to be the village of Shakespeare in Dorset.) So all is going to be all right after all. Tomorrow I am going to drive back along my route and locate that shop.

And there buy Angus a tail.

And is there honey still for tea?

Rupert Brooke
'The Old Vicarage, Grantchester'

THAT line, so evocative of the English country-
side, never fails to bring back to me the year when, as a very be-
wildered, very frightened small boy, I was evacuated to the tiny
village of Chiselbury.

Nestling like an Ovaltine advert within a grassy fold of the
Mendips, Chiselbury represents even to this day the very heart-
beat of rustic England. Just one street, one church, one pub, one
everything-shop and one Chinese takeaway. But from the moment
of my arrival there, the gentle-souled villagers took me to their
hearts, despite the fact that I was the very first wartime evacuee
they had seen. (This was because, thanks to a typically bureaucratic
excess of caution, the year was only 1935.)

They billeted me in the cottage of Mr Bowman, whose trade was
that most ancient and honourable of country crafts, wood-carving.
And many were the spellbound hours I spent watching him as,
using only a whittling-knife, his clever hands would fashion from
some unpromising log a beautifully panelled door or spiral stair-
case, perhaps even an outside-privy with heart-shaped porthole.
Sometimes, unable to restrain my childish curiosity, I would venture some question about his craft. "Mr Bowman," I'd say as the
wood-chips flew, "wouldn't it be easier if you got out of bed to
work?"

By way of answer, he would chuckle and playfully cuff my ear.
Then, relenting, he'd take his knife and from a discarded off-cut he
would whittle a little something especially for me; a wooden spoon,
perhaps, or an exquisite catapult. Even, occasionally, if he had the
time, something more elaborate – a fountain-pen or a pair of socks.

51

Mrs Bowman, his tiny and ever-smiling wife, the taste of whose cowslip-stew still comes back to me sometimes when the wind is off the Mendips, kept the village's everything-shop. And no everything-shop was ever more aptly named, for there was nothing a person could not purchase there. Milk, groceries, good country bread, ploughs, manicure sets, pianos, diving-suits, sports-cars – all the livelong day she'd be up and down the ladder fetching something or other off her many shelves. Because, besides all the other things, she also sold shelves. (And ladders.)

The third member of the Bowman household was their sixteen-year-old daughter, Annie; a strange withdrawn girl, with a great love for Nature's creatures and a forty-inch bust. So shy was she about this last attribute that she spent much of her time taking long solitary walks in the woods, accompanied only by her dog, an elderly Labrador with a matted, dank appearance like D. H. Lawrence. Sometimes, though, she would gesture me to accompany her and that, to a child of the London pavements, would indeed be a time of marvelling and wonderment.

"Oh, look, Annie!" I'd cry joyously. "Is that what they call wild honeysuckle?"

"Nay," she'd answer.

"Is it a climbing convolvulus?"

"Nay, lad."

"What is it then?"

"It's a goat." For she was wise in country-lore; sometimes we would stand motionless for whole hours at a stretch, simply so that she could observe the ways of the furred and feathered creatures that were her friends. "Sithee, lad," she'd mutter, plucking at a clump of grass, "A stoat have passed this way."

"How can you tell?" I would ask.

"Look what he done on your shoe."

Sadly, though, such was Annie's self-consciousness about her configuration, those enchanted excursions into the outer world gradually grew more and more infrequent. What finished them altogether was the morning when she washed her brassière. Having hung it out to dry on a rope between the tall trees, she came back to find two families of birds had built their nests in it. When she recognised what species of bird they were, the coincidence proved altogether too much for her.

But all that was, as the rural poet, Kern, has it, long ago and far away . . . To this day, though, there are moments when I still find myself wondering how the Bowmans are faring. Does Mr Bowman still whittle in his bed? Is Mrs Bowman still climbing up her ladder for a crêpe bandage or a two-stroke motor bike? And, perhaps the most heart-tugging question of all:

And is their Annie still forty?

There's a breathless hush in the close tonight

Sir Henry Newbolt
'Vitaï Lampada'

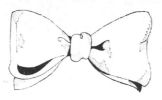

IF the poet Sir Henry Newbolt walked in on me at this moment, as the shades of night fall fast and the electric typewriter purrs like a contented cat, and asked me point blank "Are you sitting comfortably?" I would answer "Indeed I am, Sir Harry. For the first time for many a long year I am sitting without constriction, friction or loss of essential freedom."

Now any chap will confirm that this is a large claim to make. For some reason lost in antiquity the source of more discomfort and woe than anything else in a man's life is his underpant, knicker, short, brief, or whatever else you care to call his undercloth.

To begin with, why are they called 'a pair of'? We only wear one of them; the other is in the wash.

The whole history of the underpant is a harrowing story of faulty design, insufficient research and indifference to the consumer's requirements.

Why were they ever invented? Ladies went happily without the encumbrance well into the nineteenth century, taking the view that to do so would be to copy a totally masculine piece of stupidity, which would therefore be against the teachings of the Bible.

The Greeks and the Romans did not bother with underpants. On the continent of India the male underpant and the male overpant were – and often still are – the same garment.

Among the hardy Celts of North Europe the knicker was unknown. Even today your hardy Highlander disdains to wear anything beneath his kilt and suffers no vital damage, though in particularly icy weather groups of more elderly Scotsmen can be seen gathered together on the pavement grills above basement bakeries.

But then the Highlanders were a warrior people, used to foraging for months high up in the glens with just their long, heavy kilts to keep their ankles warm, and their great plaid cloaks, which they would dip into the icy waters of a burn, wring out, and wrap themselves up in for a night's sleep (this was the origin of the 'Coldstream Guards').

No, the rot seemed to have set in during the Middle Ages in the more effete parts of Central Europe, at that time almost constantly at war. The first military, pike-and-gunpowder-proof underpant was invented by a brilliant young medical scientist who made the brief out of metal. His name, after which the protective device was named, was Copperknickers (sometimes spelt Copernicus). The new garment was celebrated by Shakespeare, you will remember, in his *All's Well That End's Well*, Act II, Sc. 3; when a London merchant won a contract to make them under licence:

> Good fortune and the favour of the king
> Smile upon this contract; whose ceremony
> Shall seem expedient on the now-born brief.

The idea for making the male undergarment out of cloth came from an eighteenth-century pirate, Silver, who was a martyr to cold and wanted the garment to reach down to his ankles. As he had only one leg and found it difficult to loop the other tube of copper out of the way he caused the thing to be made out of wool and thus invented the 'Long John'.

This long woollen garment was a great success in America where new industries were rapidly expanding, often in bleak, cold, frontier regions, and the American version had refinements like long sleeves, a vent in front and an escape-hatch at the back. These facilitated industrial action and the garment became known as a 'Union' suit.

During this century the underpant has shrunk considerably in size and now barely covers the salient features. The old idea of a passion-killing one-piece still lives on, however, amongst zealous young Mormon missionaries for whom it provides a useful bulwark against amorous housewives who thought the ring on the doorbell heralded an elderly meter-reader.

My main complaint against the twentieth-century brief is not its brevity but its inefficiency. And its lack of charm.

When I was a small boy the pant was still fashioned like a pair of trousers. It was loose and baggy and itchy and did not, I submit, answer the requirements of a pant. I was forever, like Samuel Pepys, leaping aboard vehicles and sitting down only to leap up again having done myself a small but painful injury. In Pepys' case it was because the coaches of his day were badly designed; in my case it was the pant which was ill-formed.

Then came 'boxer-shorts', frightfully baggy bunches of material with an elastic waistband which left the tummy crimped. And 'Y-Fronts', a breakthrough as regards industrial design but unsatisfactory as regards material – it was like being wrapped in an old vest.

In desperation I turned to the really brief 'briefs'. These came from the continent of Europe and bore names like 'Señor' and 'Hercule'. They arrived in three sizes: too small, too large, and medium. I wore 'medium', which were too small when I bought them and too large after two washes.

Why, oh why, I asked myself – as millions of chaps have asked themselves over the centuries – does our underwear have to be so *harsh*? The brief is the best of the bunch by a mile but is so unsympathetic. The elastic of the legs leaves weals on the upper thighs if it is to do its job and the cotton fabric rubs.

I resolved to solve the problem and begin from first principles. I went to Egham and bought a square yard of material which, clearly, lacked harshness; fine towelling. It had thousands of little cotton ears on it which made it soft. I bore it home and applied it to my nude person. I studied the geometry of the problem first, folded the square into a triangle and wrapped the hypotenuse round my waist. I then bent down and dragged the corner of the triangle forwards and upwards between my legs and fastened it, together with the ends of the hypotenuse, with a safety-pin. So far so good, but not far enough. The whole thing tended to swivel when I moved about. It was unstable. It needed anchorage. But to where?

The tummy-button is a much underestimated part of the human body. It is there, collecting fluff, but it is seldom put to use. Perhaps this is because of folklore. I believed – until humiliatingly recently – that if you unscrewed your tummy-button your bottom fell off. But the fact is that the tummy-button is there to be used if a use can be found.

I found the use. I nipped out into the garden and selected a tiny conker from beneath the horse-chestnut tree. I pierced the conker with a skewer and threaded a piece of string through it, tying the string to a safety-pin. Folding my non-harsh towelling about my person, I clasped the whole thing tightly about my waist and fastened the three corners with the conker-attached safety-pin, conker inwards.

You see the beauty – and truth – of my Creative Thinking? The conker nestled happily in my tummy-button like a ball in a socket; flexible, pliant, answering to my every movement yet anchoring the soft, towelling brief.

Which is why if Sir Henry Newbolt walked in and asked me "Are you sitting comfortably?" I would reply "Indeed I am, Sir Hal. It may not be immediately apparent as I am fully dressed, but beneath . . .?

"There's a brief, less harsh, in the clothes tonight."

You can't have your cake and eat it too

Proverb
Heywood

HAVE you noticed that although people who've been pronounced innocent in court cases frequently proclaim the verdict "a vindication of British Justice", you very rarely hear anyone say that when he's been found guilty?

The reason that I didn't say it on the only occasion I was sent down for a number of serious offences was not because the verdict was unfair – which it was – but because I only had myself to blame. So convinced had I been that the judge would immediately throw the whole series of trumped-up charges out of court, I'd decided to conduct my own defence.

Oh, I admit that the ridiculous accusations which the woman had brought against me may have sounded bad – and, at the time of the incident, they might even have looked pretty bad, too – but, as I tried to explain to His Lordship, that kind of thing can so easily happen with contact-lenses. Especially when you've only been wearing them for a week, which is all I'd had them in for when my Lodge held their Ladies Night Dinner & Dance.

Well, you're all reasonable people – having now heard my defence, wouldn't you have dismissed all the charges against me and sent me forth with no stain on my character and costs awarded for loss of working time? I can only tell you – not him. Not that old poop sitting up there in moth-eaten glory. He just pouted his lips and said, "Mr Norden, I have not the faintest idea what you are talking about."

So off we were obliged to launch into all the irrelevant details, wasting the court's time and the taxpayers' money with a whole mass of interminable argy-bargy. As patiently as I could I described how, on the night in question, the woman and I had just finished dancing an Excuse-Me tango when I noticed that the right-hand side of the ballroom seemed to be in much clearer focus than the left-hand side.

Well, I twigged immediately what must have happened. Some time during the course of our dance, probably while I was moving her into one of my Valentino bend-overs, my left-hand contact-lens had dislodged itself and fallen. There being no sign of it on the highly-polished floor, the only other landing-ground had to be my partner's dress. As the top of that garment featured what I believe is called a Boat Neck – in her case, of battleship proportions – that was obviously the first place to start searching.

All right, I concede that – arguably – I should perhaps have mentioned my intentions to the woman before attempting to re-trieve the missing article. But, by the same token, I must disabuse you of any notion that I straightaway pulled up my sleeve, shoved an arm down and proceeded to grub around for the little sliver of plastic. On the contrary. In the most gentlemanly way possible, I simply positioned myself behind her, clasped both her shoulders, put a knee in her back and then – for no more than at most forty seconds – agitated her upper body in a rapid rotatory movement. Sure enough, my lost lens was shaken from its hiding-place and slid down to the floor.

That's really all there was to it. Be honest now, does it by any stretch of imagination constitute grounds for charging a person with grievous bodily harm, indecent assault and loss of conjugal benefit? That last enormity, by the way, was piled on by her hus-band, because – so he alleged – ever since the incident, not only did she throw a wobbly at the slightest murmur of tango rhythms, even the sight of a piano-accordion brought her out in hives. That being so, he averred, she was now rendered incapable of partnering him in their attempt on the forthcoming Southern Area Latin American Championships, so he was asking for punitive damages in the sum of £3,000, plus the cost of a wasted beehive wig.

Even to a layman, their entire case was so patently lacking in substance I had no hesitation at all in deciding to act as my own advocate. What's more, it soon became obvious that the barrister my opponents had hired – as foxy-looking a shyster as I've seen this side of Elisha Cook Jnr – was indulging in tactics that would have got him disbarred in a banana republic. After a few establishing questions to the wife, he had the usher put on a Victor Sylvester recording of *Jealousy* – then, to and fro across the well of the court, he and his client danced to it; his object being, of course, to demonstrate proof of the marked deterioration in her tango-ing faculties.

I let them do a full thirty-two bars before I released my shaft. Rising to my feet and pointing to the cavorting couple, "Your Lordship," I said, "I object."

"Why do you object?" said the judge.

"On the ground that Counsel is *leading* the witness."

The judge's response was to adjourn the court for lunch. Although, at the time, I viewed that as points to my side, it was actually the move which led to my downfall.

You see, in my ignorance of the law, what I'd failed to realise was that courtroom lunch-breaks only last from one o'clock till two. So instead of making for the canteen, I remained in my seat writing up some notes on the case with a view to getting them included in the BBC series 'Great Advocates Of Our Time'. It was only when I noticed the judge returning to his high-chair that I realised we were kicking off again and I hadn't had a thing to eat. All I could do was grab a hunk of cold bread-pudding I happened to be carrying in my brief-case and wolf it down.

Well, you've probably guessed the result. When I was called on to deliver my final masterly summing-up for the defence, I found myself overcome by such a grotesque attack of hiccups, I could only thump my chest wildly and shake my head. Taking this as a gesture of surrender, Your Lordship stopped the case and awarded judgment for the plaintiffs.

So, although I cannot in all fairness point an accusing finger at the workings of British Justice, I do have reservations about its meal-times. Put it another way: if you ever decide to act as your own defence counsel, you must above all things make sure you get in the canteen-queue sharp at one.

Put it yet a third way:

You can't advocate and eat at two.

The game is up

Shakespeare
Cymbeline, Act III, Sc. 3

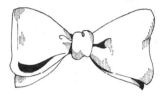

I propose to make a million pounds or so in the coming months by writing a best-seller, a romantic novel of the type known to hospital-library trolley-pushers and librarians as Light Love.

This will mean writing under a nom-de-plume, of course, but this is quite usual. It may come as something of a shock to you but Eleanor Papworthy (*Daddy Blue-Eyes, Sigh No More Stranger, Dimples*, etc.) is a retired accountant whose real name is Arthur Fosset. And Monica Lavender (*Beloved Rogue, For the Love of a King, The Passionate Quaker*, etc., etc.) is bearded and before striking it rich was a riveter in a Clyde shipyard. My romantic novel will be written under the pen-name of 'Deborah Horseland'. This should keep me just ahead of Barbara Cartland.

After studying a number of these novels and giving the matter a good deal of thought – I spent almost the whole of last Tuesday on it – I have come up with a winner of a plot. It has all the elements which are most successful in the genre; an historical setting, aristocracy, low life, dark doings in the past and a hero who is ideal for the heroine.

The heroine's mother is a ravishing Society beauty married to an elderly politician. I call her Lady Caroline Mutton because she is like a slightly older Lady Caroline Lamb. Lady Caroline had been a bit of a goer in her youth and had had a steamy ding-dong with an impoverished poet which resulted in the birth of our heroine. I call Lady Caroline's lover Thomas Tupper – a little joke for my sheep-farmer readers.

As was usual in those days our baby heroine is smuggled away and put out to a wet-nurse (whatever that is – I'll look it up). Lady Caroline disguises herself as a trollop (we all know what that is) and does the rounds of the taverns to find foster-parents for the infant. This will give me the opportunity to indulge in some fine descriptive writing of Georgian London: squeaking inn-signs, "Won't you buy my sweet fresh lavender, kind lady?", one-legged beggars, stage-coaches setting off for Inverness (or somewhere. I'll check where they went), Bow-Street Runners, all that sort of rubbish.

In a tavern in Maiden Lane (singularly inappropriate Lane come to think of it – I'll change it later) over against a music shop ('over against' means 'next to': it is the sort of period phrase I will go in for strongly: they used 'over against' in the old days because most of the houses in Olde London fell over and rested against the house next door) Lady Caroline meets the owner of the shop, a kindly old retired musician named Jabez Harp. She strikes a bargain and for a guinea-and-a-half he undertakes to adopt the child and bring her up as his own. Lady Caroline then downs a swift port-and-lemon and disappears from his life and our story.

We then jump a few years and pick up where our heroine is sweet seventeen and a picture to behold and here I anticipate running into trouble. How do you describe a heroine except to state that she has an oval face? What alternative shape of face *could* she have? Rectangular? Square? And all heroines seem to have hazel eyes, i.e. eyes like a small nut (I'll work something out).

She has grown up into a happy young woman, always dashing about laughing and cheering people up. When the wind used to blow, and the house used to lean even further against the tavern next door, to the terror of Jabez and his good wife, the girl would laugh and cheer them up with a song. So they christened her Aeolian Harp.

With her merry laughter and her stunning good looks Aeolian becomes an actress. She joins the company of the celebrated actor, George Frederick Cooke, and goes with the company on a tour of the provinces (this is the origin of Cooke's Tours).

But all does not go well on tour. Aeolian's acting is not bad but her jollity becomes a little wearing on the nerves of the cast. The first to crack is George Frederick Cooke himself. After a disastrous week in Scunthorpe he announces to the company that the total week's takings are three shillings and twopence.

"Never mind, love," cries Aeolian, bursting into a trill of laughter, "the play's the thing!"

He walks out, takes to drink and becomes one of the most spectacular drunks in the history of British theatre (quite true).

The next to crack is the saturnine, wild-eyed but exceedingly handsome juvenile lead Jemmy Trotter (our hero). This is not his real name. He is really young Lord Battersea who has been temporarily diddled out of his stately home and inheritance by somebody-or-other for a reason I'll work out later and has taken to the stage incognito to earn his living.

He falls in love with Aeolian, and vice-versa, one afternoon when he blunders in while she is changing her costume. This will be a chance for a touch of 'her magnificent bare bosoms heaved as though his piercing eyes were exercising some spell upon them. With a faint cry she modestly covered her face with her hands as his breath, now so hot that the varnish on her dressing-room door began to bubble . . .' (they like a fair amount of this sort of stuff in Light Love as long as nobody actually *does* anything). But her unremitting jollity and stentorian laugh rapidly wear away his ardour and two days later he leaves and joins the Navy.

Aeolian, heartbroken, also leaves the stage and becomes a Kept Woman (it's all right; I'll make her protector an old merchant aged about a hundred and four who only wants her for a tax-loss, or something like that). But one evening, when she is trying to cheer him up, her laugh shatters a priceless chandelier and she is flung out on her ear.

We next find her, destitute, hungry, being frog-marched out of a Revivalist Mission for laughing during Charles Wesley's sermon.

She decides to end it all by throwing herself over the Embankment into the cold, dark waters of the Thames (if there *was* an Embankment in those days. If not, over Chelsea Bridge. If that was not there either, off the top of the Tower of London).

Meanwhile our hero, Jemmy Trotter, has got on well in the Navy and is a captain. Unhappily he has a nasty accident and is invalided out. One day Nelson asks him to go and get the gunnery officer, Lieutenant Farr. Not knowing which gun the Lieutenant is working on, Jemmy shoves his head down the first gun-barrel he comes across and yells "Farr!!" The cannon-ball hits him on the head but misses anything vital so he lives. The only damage is to his hearing, which is permanently impaired. But Fate smiles upon him. Whoever-it-was who had nicked his title and fortune comes to some sort of bad end and it is as wealthy Lord Battersea that he strolls that evening along the Embankment (or across Chelsea Bridge, or over the roof of the Tower of London) in time to stop his one true love from hurling herself into the waters.

"Aeolian!" he cries, clasping her to him, "I thank merciful Heaven that I found you in time. We will wed this very minute. There is an Off-Licence in Caxton Hall who will make us one!" (This ending is a bit like *Fanny Hill* but I think the readership of the two books will be sufficiently different for the rip-off to go unnoticed.)

"I am so happy!" she cries, and bursts into the loudest laughter she has ever laughed.

But the noise of her laughter does not bother him one bit. Theirs will be a truly happy marriage, however bright her merriment or cheerful her laughter, because, of course, her dear husband is stone deaf.

Good story, isn't it?

And I have found just the right title. Her name, with a description of her main characteristic, and a slight period flavour. I am going to call it:

The Gay Miss Harp.

Beggars can't be choosers

Proverb

AFTER Monsieur Lafarge had introduced me to his colleagues, he explained the problem which the Calais Chamber of Commerce had brought me over to solve. "What our town has become," he said gloomily, "is a sort of geographical revolving-door. A place many people pass through but no one ever thinks of staying inside."

I appreciated their predicament. For millions of British holiday-makers, the name Calais means little more than a port-of-entry for driving towards other Continental watering-places, or a port-of-departure for catching the car-ferry back to England. The truth, however, is that this pleasant seaside town has much to offer the English visitor, including attractive beaches, excellent local dishes, excursions to many places of interest and, in my case, a whacking down-payment on the fee, balance to be handed over in hundred-franc notes, no questions asked and blow the VAT. Provided, that is, provided I could dream up some novelty attraction that would induce my fellow-countrymen to linger round the dump for an extra few days. . . .

The first idea I put to the Chamber was the obvious one – capitalise on the town's well-established historical links with the U.K. After all, if there's one history lesson that every British school-child has dozed over, it's that episode about 'the burghers of Calais': those six old-timers Edward the Third threatened to string up with their own ropes. "So the thing to do," I instructed the assembled merchants, "is play-up your historical assets. The shop-keepers among you must stop presenting yourselves to English visitors as retail-stockists or distributor-outlets. From now on, you've all got to be 'burghers'. That's where the money is. Is there a butcher here?" Monsieur Hippolyte raised his hand. "Right," I said. "You be the beef-burgher. The chap who runs the dairy can be the cheese-burgher. And if any of you are in the local Amateur Dramatic society –?" No less than four hands went up. "Fine," I said, "Ham-burghers."

I was really warming to it now. "Tell you what," I said, "You four can help push the history tie-up even further. For a really dead-cert tourist grabber, how about we put on a 'Son et Lumière' presentation in the Main Square, re-enacting that whole Edward the Third scenario throughout the holiday season?'

Everyone received the idea so enthusiastically it really should have worked, especially as it cost nearly as much as *A Bridge Too Far* to produce and I went to no end of trouble writing the script. What I neglected to bear in mind, however, was that a 'Son et Lumière' differs from a situation-comedy in two vital respects. First, it has to be done in the open air; second, you have to stage it in darkness, at night. As the road alongside the Main Square is the principal highway to the Cote d'Azur, the whole 'Son' part of the 'Son et Lumière' got drowned-out by a procession of GB-plate drivers putting their foot down so as to get to Lyons before breakfast. And as for the 'Lumière' – well, that blinked out for good when the only British vehicle that did pause to watch – a four-berth caravan – parked smack on the power cables.

Fortunately, I have never been one to let a mere disaster upset me. "Not to worry," I said, surveying the despondent faces at the next Chamber of Commerce meeting. "There's more than one way for a seaside resort to pull in passing trade. Know what lots of British places have been finding surefire? A Beauty Contest! 'Miss Bridlington', 'Miss Jaywick Sands' – that sort of thing. Just vote me a few hundred thousand francs more for publicity, and I promise you – this time next month you'll be worrying about a shortage of hotel rooms."

Well, the moment the money was okayed, I started working like a demon. By the following Monday morning, there wasn't one roadway leading out of the dock area that didn't bear an enormous placard that read 'All this week – MISS CALAIS!'

The trouble was, every English driver coming off the ferry read it as an *instruction*.

The next time I met with the city elders there were distinct signs of what my mother calls 'an atmosphere'. I couldn't help but notice every one of them was looking at me as though I was in direct line-of-descent from Edward the Third. Monsieur Lafarge set the pace. "Mr Norden," he said, "the feeling of the meeting is that we are just playing silly burghers."

"D'accord," Monsieur Duval said. "In spite of all the money we have spent and the exorbitant fee you have charged us, our beaches are still deserted.'

"More to the point," said Monsieur Aznavour (I asked him but he said he wasn't), "all our town has left in its coffers now is thirty francs. And, Mr Norden, there is no possible way that anyone can suddenly throng an empty resort by an expenditure of thirty francs."

Well, if there's one thing calculated to bring out the best in me, it's a challenge. I tell you, I positively *felt* my nostrils flare. "Monsieur Racine," I said to the local printer, "would thirty francs buy me just one more road-sign? Just a little one?"

Grudgingly, he nodded. And that nod is the reason why, today, a gratifying 83 per cent of those British cars that used to roar straight through Calais now make a sudden left-hand turn when they reach the dock gateway and follow the road indicated by the arrow on my little sign. A sign that is nevertheless large enough for the seven words above the arrow to be read by an oncoming driver: 'This Way To The Nude Bathing Beaches'.

Months later, in the speech I made graciously turning down the Chamber of Commerce's offer of a statue in the Main Square, I pointed out that I had already received my sufficient reward. That came in the form of the *Calais Observateur*'s front-page photograph of Messieurs Hippolyte, Lafarge and Racine standing by the breakwater, all busily using pocket-calculators to try and estimate how many thousands of British holidaymakers were wandering the sands in search of uncovered skin.

The caption beneath it, though it loses a little in translation, had a simple eloquence:
BURGHERS COUNT BEACH-USERS.

It is better to travel hopefully than to arrive

Proverbial saying derived from a line
by Robert Louis Stevenson

A most extraordinary thing has happened to our household. After many years of being dog-people – first poodles and then Afghans – we have taken to cats. Once doggy we are now moggy. We have become transmogrified.

Our cats are Burmese which might explain a lot; Burmese cats tend to be individuals rather than members of the Cat Family. They have given us so much pleasure that I was tempted to do a rave about their beauty and companionship and sense of fun but I think a better picture will emerge of living with cats if I just drivel on about random incidents.

I first met a Burmese cat when we were having lunch at the home of a chap called Andrew Lloyd-Webber who writes music. After lunch we sat around discussing things like semi-quavers and royalties when a smallish, dark-brown cat strode in, summed up in a flash that I was not a cat-fancier, sprang lightly onto my lap, curled up and composed himself to slumber. It was like having a mink-covered hot-water bottle on one. When I rose to go he rose with me, transferring himself to my shoulder. When we left our host had to detach him from me by levering him off with a cello bow. Such affection was a rare experience.

My own Burmese kitten, Kettering (named after a town in Northants where lives a nice publisher) arrived on my birthday. I was in bed with a cold at the time. A cardboard box was presented to me by the family. Books? I wondered. Soap? A woolly garment? I opened the top of the box and a small, chocolate-coloured head emerged. Huge, round, yellow-Chartreuse eyes looked at me levelly. He skipped lightly out of the box and curled himself up

68

round my adam's apple for the day.

With two Afghan ladies of some age on the premises we had a problem. The inborn instinct of a hound is to chase and kill small furry beasts. They could not believe their luck that they had been presented with a resident quarry. They hurled themselves at the bedroom door to get at Kettering. They tried to tunnel under the door. We resolved on a system of apartheid until we could resolve the problem. The kitten lived during the day safely amid the springs of the bed. The dogs were kept downstairs.

On advice I telephoned the chief veterinary officer of one of our animal charities. He seemed a good bet as he owned Afghans himself.

"I wish to introduce a Burmese kitten into a household which includes two Afghans," I began.

"A *kitten!*" he said. "You've got two Afghans and now you've gone and got a kitten! Oh, my goodness! Oh deary, deary me! Oh, my goodness, you *have* got a problem! Oh, Gawd! . . ." That was the sum total of his professional advice.

I built a strong wire cage, like a huge rat-trap. We inserted a protesting Kettering into this every evening and took it downstairs so that the dogs would get used to him and realise that he had come to stay and was one of the family (we read that in a book). The dogs knocked us out of the way and tried to bite through the wire. Kettering was relatively unmoved. He sat and glared at them and if a nose was pushed through the bars he swatted it with a paw.

It took four nerve-wracked months but eventually the natural lethargy of living things took over and the dogs ceased to care all that much. A guarded form of peaceful co-existence came into being and it became accepted by all three that as long as there was no food about there would be no war. They walked warily past each other but there was no aggro.

At Christmas my wife's kitten arrived. Also in a cardboard box. He is called Monticello (after a village in Corsica) and is silver (i.e. grey) with a beautiful face, a raucous little voice and a fat tummy. His first meeting with an Afghan was interesting. He took one look at the great shaggy face looming over him, hauled off and let loose a right hook that would have felled an ox. The Afghan staggered away, gloomily contemplating the sad turn of world events.

It must be admitted that cats, unlike dogs, tend to shred the

69

house a little. We have hessian wallpaper in the dining room and both cats like to show off when strangers are present and run up the wall. They also occasionally run up the curtains, stroll along the mantelpiece brushing the ornaments off the edge, hide in the kitchen cupboards and induce heart failure in somebody innocently reaching for a saucepan, and sit on one's paper when one is trying to write a letter.

Their need to unsheath their scimitars and lock onto one's clothing when being carried about means that threads are drawn. All my jackets are now covered in tiny fairy croquet-hoops.

Both cats sleep in our bed. This is quite indefensible on all grounds. It is not only unhygienic but downright dangerous. But how do you keep them out? They wait until you are asleep and then in they come, burrowing down to the bottom of the bed and then easing their way up until they find a warm nook or cranny. And they shift around during the night, unloosing the scimitars and having a good scratch at anything to hand. They rarely draw blood but they leave distinct weals in the flesh. When I had my first bath after the arrival of Kettering I saw my back in the mirror and I looked like a steel engraving from Foxe's *Book of Martyrs*.

I do not normally wear pyjamas and it seemed to me that now was the time to start, so, in self-protection, I wore a pair of pyjama bottoms. It was a grave error. There is nothing a kitten likes more than running up a tunnel.

What *is* it about cats that so intrigues? The French painter Méry wrote that cats were God's way of permitting man to caress a tiger. There is something in this but it does not stand up to close scrutiny. Caressing a tiger (or, at least, caressing a cheetah, which I have done) is like stroking a pig the wrong way. Caressing a Burmese cat is like stroking velvet. Cats walk in a beautiful, loping, tiger-like stride but when they run their bottoms seem to be trying to overtake them and they wobble from side to side in a most untigerlike fashion.

I suppose it comes down to trying to work out what cats are thinking about behind that shining, opaque stare. The theory is that cats know a hell of a lot but do not let on. I wonder. But perhaps wondering what goes on inside cats' noddles is what makes them seem not only beautiful and graceful but mysterious and enigmatic; a perpetual mystery.

Sorry this piece has not been more organised but as I said at the beginning I wanted to drivel on and, I hope, sketch in a picture of what living with cats means.

In a case like this I rather agree with Robert Louis Stevenson's thought:

It is better to drivel hopefully than do a rave.

Where are the snows of yesteryear?

François Villon

WHAT finally persuaded me I should have the operation was brandy-balloons; even though they represent only one of the embarrassments you encounter when you've got a big nose. A brandy-balloon is a drinking-glass with a large, voluptuously-shaped bowl that curves round to an extremely narrow rim – think of a fat avocado with the tip sliced off – but what happens when an extravagantly-beaked person drinks from such a goblet is that the moment his lips meet the near edge of the narrow rim, he finds his nose-tip is already jamming against the far edge. In consequence, it becomes quite impossible for him to get any kind of *tilt* on the balloon. When you remember that the brandy itself sits down at the bottom of it, that leaves a large-hootered person like myself only two options. I either have to ask my host if he'd please fill my glass right up to the brim or, failing that, bring out a straw. Both these alternatives get you talked about.

It was that kind of sociàl discomfiture which led me to consider having what's called a 'nose-job'. What clinched it for me was reading in one of the Sunday supplements that this particular technique of cosmetic surgery has become such a doddle, you can now have your facial irregularity replaced by any shape or size of nose you fancy. I immediately contacted my secretary and asked her to send away for a Nose Catalogue.

Whether she was unfamiliar with medical procedures or whether she simply misheard me I don't know, but all I received by return of post was a highly-coloured brochure offering me a choice of standard, miniature, climbing or floribunda. So I got out the Yellow Pages, let my fingers do some jogging up the column marked Surgeons (Cosmetic), made a phone-call and fixed an appointment.

He was one of those black-jacket-and-striped-trouser types who probably looked like a boardroom portrait while still a child, but he was affable enough and after we'd agreed on a model that would blend with the rest of my facial environment, he said, "Fine. Now, when we've got you under, is there any other malformation you'd like corrected?" Somewhat on the principle, I thought, that a house-decorator will say, "While I'm up the ladder, want me to have a look at your guttering as well?"

"No thanks," I said. "Apart from the Cyrano, I think Nature has been reasonably kind.' He inspected me searchingly. "Your ears are a bit sticking-out."

I'd forgotten about them. They do project somewhat; to an extent, in fact, that with my hair cut short, I bear a distinct face-on resemblance to the F.A. Cup. "All right then," I agreed, "perhaps you'd better give them just a slight pinning-back."

"Sure there's nothing else?"

I pondered. "Come to think of it," I said. "Every time I'm measured for a sports-jacket, they tell me my left shoulder is about an inch-and-a-half higher than the right." He made a note of it. "Oh, and another thing that's just come back to me. The chap in the shirt shop always says my right arm is a good three-quarters of an inch longer than the left."

He turned over a fresh page of his order-book. "That the lot?"

"Not quite," I said, warming to it now. "For some reason I take a size 10½ shoe on one foot but an 11 on the other. And there was something else. What was it? . . . Oh yes. My inside-leg measurements."

"What about them?" he said.

"Well, I don't quite understand this, but for some reason they're longer than my outside-leg measurements."

He closed his book. "I think I'd better send you an estimate."

You'll never believe what he quoted me for the full service. £400! Naturally I queried it with him but he showed me a complete item-by-item breakdown of his costings and that does seem to be what this kind of job comes to nowadays. It's not the parts, you see, it's the labour.

But £400! I went straight home, sat down in front of the shaving mirror and made another long hard appraisal of the nose. Is it really all that awful? Well, not really. Certainly not by comparison with – no, I'd better not mention her name. Oh, admittedly it's looking a bit pointier and pinchier with every passing decade – but even so, there's still quite a bit of mileage there before it gets to be truly grotesque. All things considered, I'll stay with it.

So have I now completely discarded the idea of having a trumpet-trim? Not entirely. If I ever win the National Lottery, it would probably still be the first thing I'd lash out largesse on. But until then – well, at £400 a throw, my thinking has to be the same as François Villon's:

Wear out the shnozz of yesteryear.

He jests at scars that never felt a wound

Shakespeare
Romeo and Juliet, Act ii, Sc. 2

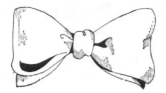

I was once very fond of Romeo and Juliet but they were too expensive for me and I changed to those little cigars that come five to a tin, like pilchards. They were not so nice to smoke but were probably nicer than smoking pilchards.

I became a cigar-smoker by chance some ten years ago. It was late in December and I remember wondering what I would get for Christmas. I had a shrewd idea that I would be getting either a street-map of the suburbs of Melbourne, an oboe reed or a jar of pickled walnuts. I am sometimes psychic in matters like these.

When Christmas came do you know what I got? Virus pneumonia. That was not all I got for Christmas, of course. I also got pleurisy.

It was not a very jolly Christmas for any of us. I ran a very high temperature and just lay flat, seeing faces in the wallpaper and steaming like a Christmas pudding. It was particularly arduous for my family. That Christmas was the coldest for years and it was a great labour for them to keep trundling me from room to room to warm the house up.

When it was all over I had an interview with my chest specialist in Harley Street.

"Do you want the bad news first?" he asked quietly.

I went suddenly cold. "Yes . . . yes, of course. Let me have it straight."

His eyes were full of compassion as, wordlessly, he passed me an envelope containing an account of his fees.

"And the good news?" I ventured.

'You are now perfectly healthy. Just give up smoking cigarettes from now on. O.K.?"

Give up smoking cigarettes? No problem to a person of my mental calibre and powers of self-discipline I assured myself. I turned over in my mind all the previous things I had managed to give up: ice-skating, the burnt currents in rice-pudding, Proust, Party Political Broadcasts, yoghourt, Charlie Chaplin films, striped toothpaste, pyjamas, hitch-hiking, sliced bread, waistcoats, Mrs Mary Whitehouse, toasted tea-cakes, turnups on trousers, weeding the garden, queueing, the novels of C. P. Snow, going for a bracing walk, fried onions, Y-Front pants, rice and 'Stars on Sunday'. But then a horrible truth made itself apparent; these were things I *wanted* to give up. I did not want to give up cigarettes.

What followed was a nightmare. As soon as the trembling hand reached for a packet of the forbidden weed I forced it back. I felt I was going mad, losing weight, falling apart. I kept telling myself that I *will* give up cigarettes, that as soon as I can begin to give them up then pride will strengthen my resolve. I went hot and cold alternately as I strove to break a deeply-entrenched habit. I developed a twitch. Was impatient, lost my knack of touching problems lightly and being a source of comfort to others. I developed a morbid conviction that my elbows were growing like weeds. That my fingernails itched. Finally I could take no more. I went back to the specialist and said, "I can't do it! I've tried! God knows I've tried! But I just can't give them up!"

He said, "You've only been as far as the front door and back. Give it a bit longer. If you want to you can smoke the occasional cigar."

I wrung his hand in gratitude and made my way home.

And so I began to smoke the occasional cigar. With immense difficulty.

The trouble with cigars is how to light them. There was no such trouble with cigarettes. One touched a flame to one end, sucked on the other and various chemicals ensured that the things stayed alight. The chemicals were more obvious in French cigarettes which fizzed away like sparklers, going 'snap', 'crackle' and 'pop'. A big cigar is another matter entirely. It rests in your hand like a deeply-bronzed banana. And unlike the humble cigarette, it is only open at one end. The end you shove in your mouth is closed up with folded leaves, like the blunt end of an onion.

76

In the Hollywood films of my youth Edward G. Robinson seemed to have no trouble in coping with this blunt end. As Betty Grable, bespangled, the famous legs clad in bullet-proof tights, took to the speakeasy stage to begin her hit number Edward G. bit into the end of his cigar, spat and applied match.

I think that you have to have the teeth for it. My front teeth do not quite match up in the middle. This means that I cannot easily eat corn on the cob. What I have to do is hold the cob and force each corn against the chisel surface of a specific tooth and lever away, one corn at a time. When I tried to bite the end off my cigar there was a crunching sound and I had a mouthful of what tasted like dead cabbage leaves.

I tried pushing a matchstick into the end to make a hole and sawing off the end with a penknife, but in each case I ended up with the thing unrolling itself and coming to rest in my palm rather like one of those bars of flaky chocolate.

I then tried moving away from big, real cigars into those tiny cigar-substitutes. The difficulty was keeping those alight. They lit readily but invariably went out half-way through. I found myself a victim of mid-whiffery.

Cigars are a mockery, I cried. Why cannot there be some system of smoking cigar tobacco as one smokes a pipe? Pipes do not un-roll in one's palm, or need biting beforehand. They smoke evenly and placidly.

The answer to my prayers came to me in a Magic Shop. That is to say, a shop devoted to selling conjuring tricks and similar para-phernalia. I had gone into the shop to purchase a squirting carna-tion or, as the sign said, a 'Joke Button-Hole: Just Wait for The Laffs When Your Buddies Bend Down to Sniff Your Boutonniere!' I needed this to solve a small problem I found when travelling home by train from Waterloo station to Egham. I would nip into the station buffet and order a cup of coffee. When it arrived (if it arrived at all) it was usually steaming hot and undrinkable for eight minutes whereas my train was due to arrive in five minutes. I reckoned that if I had a Joke Squirting Buttonhole I could lean towards the hot coffee and, without bringing embarrassment upon myself, squirt the little rubber bulb and direct a stream of cold water into the coffee. Anyway, while I was in the Magic Shop I suddenly saw for sale an all-purpose Magic Wand. A thin wooden cylinder, painted black with white ends, into which the aspiring

77

magician could stuff flags, silk handkerchiefs, fried eggs, in fact anything which he could then produce at will and amaze his friends. Inspiration struck. I bought four Magic Wands.

It was the work of but a few moments to carve a mouthpiece in the soft wood of the Wands. A cigar, unrolled, provided enough tobacco to fill three Wands. They lit beautifully, like a fine meerschaum pipe, and burnt steadily. I had found a perfect compromise between the efficiency of a pipe and the farce of trying to light a cigar.

I now no longer make mock of the dark-brown leaf. As Shakespeare almost said:

He jests at cigars who never filled a wand.

They make a desert and they call it peace

Tacitus
'Agricola'

YOU ready to hear something really chilling? Not long ago, a distinguished thinker hit upon the most profound philosophical statement ever revealed to mankind, then had to discard it because it wouldn't fit on a T-shirt.

I found that just one more piece of supporting evidence for my theory that if the nineteen-seventies do go down in history – and we're agreed, aren't we, that they are unlikely to go up – the decade will almost certainly be remembered as The T-shirt Years. Every person under the age of forty-five is taking on the appearance of an ambulant billboard. Wherever you turn, emblazoned singlets display multi-coloured full-face portraits of today's Culture Heroes – Solzhenitsyn, Kurt Vonnegut, Laurel and Hardy – or else they exhibit slogans embodying every kind of contemporary preoccupation. These range from the boldly partisan ('Boadicea Lives!'; 'Bring Back The Cod-Piece!') to the politically extreme ('Keep Foreigners Out Of The Common Market'; 'Put Betting Shops On The National Health'). From the ethically questionable ('Love Is A Many Gendered Thing'; 'Sex Leads To Housework') to the downright incomprehensible ('The Truth Lies Somewhere In-Between'; 'Keep On The Grass').

Until quite recently, though, this transformation of the population into human hoardings was something I viewed with little more than resigned tolerance. ("I may not agree with what your T-shirt says but I will fight to the death for your right to wear it.") Then something happened that changed my attitude significantly. One of the major networks made us a handsome offer to put the 'My Word!' series on television.

We could perform it, they promised, in exactly the same form as we were accustomed to doing it on radio, except – and here I quote from the eager-shirted young producer ('Social Consciousness Is Not Enough') they sent round – "except for one minor alteration". Apparently the average viewer is not what the young man kept calling "verbally orientated", so something would have to be done to give the televised version of the programme – and again I use quotation-marks to indicate his exact words – "more pace".

"Take those quotations you and Frank build your stories round," he argued. 'Your average telly-addict would never be able to retain them in his mind all the while you're rabbiting. If we're going to hold his interest, maintain the pace he's got used to in *Starsky and Hutch*, we've really got to provide Joe Public with some sort of ongoing visual reference-point.'

Thoughtfully, Frank took out his chased-silver snuff-box. "Such as like what?" he asked softly.

"Nothing you need worry yourself about, baby," the producer said, slapping him genially on the shoulder – never a wise thing to do while Frank is taking snuff. After we'd cleaned Frank's ears, the youth outlined his proposed revisions. During that portion of the programme in which the two stories are recounted, Dilys Powell, the lady who sits at Frank's side, would wear a T-shirt on which would be embroidered whatever quotation he was weaving his magic on; similarly, when it came to my turn, my partner Anne Scott-James would be seen in a T-shirt bearing the line I was working on.

"Get the visual impact?" he enquired eagerly. "All the time either of you is labouring his way through to the pay-off line, there – right next to you – is someone showing exactly what your target is. All kidding aside, fellers, it'll make that whole long-winded section go like a chase-sequence! . . . Do me a favour," he said as he noticed our faces, "at least think about it."

How can one think about the unthinkable? How is it possible to consider the inconceivable? Without getting too rhetorical, let me simply ask you to recall the Pepys quotation with which Frank was lumbered a scant few weeks back. In all honesty, can you really imagine Dilys Powell – our delicate, softly-spoken Dilys – can you imagine her clad in a white cotton singlet that reads 'And So To Bed'?

While Anne – the handsome, invincibly elegant Lady Scott-

James – to put her in any kind of T-shirt can only be compared to draping bunting over the dome of St Paul's. As for embossing one of my quotations across it – could anyone really want to see Anne-Scott-James sitting with her noble upper-half covered in something that reads 'These Are A Few Of My Favourite Things'?

No, it's simply not on, is it? Typical though, I suppose. Typical both of the contemporary mania for communicating by means of an embroidered under-vest and Television's obsession with speeding-up everything it touches. Funny how nearly right old Tacitus got it:

They make a T-shirt and they call it 'pace'.

The workers have nothing to lose but their chains

Communist Manifesto

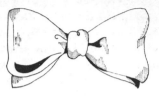

QUITE by accident I have stumbled upon a theory which could well turn the art world topsy-turvy and call for an entirely new approach to exhibitions, art histories and *catalogues raisonnés* (catalogues with raisins in them).

It all came about when I received a very flattering phone call asking me to paint a picture for a local art exhibition to be put on by the Runnymede Art Society, of which I am president. The chap on the phone said that the theme of the exhibition was Florence Nightingale.

I had never painted a picture before so I had no canvases but I found an old tarpaulin in the garden which my aunty used to cover her motorbike. It was about eight feet by six feet, just the right size for an impressive oil painting, so I stretched it out and nailed it to the garage door. I sat down and had a think about what exactly I was going to paint. If I had heard the chap on the phone correctly the picture had to represent some aspect of Florence. At night. In a gale. No problem – only a few days previously I had received a picture postcard of Florence from my aunty who had gone to stay there for a couple of months while her hair returned to its natural colour. I went and fetched the postcard. It was a fine view of the cathedral, topped by Brunelleschi's mighty dome. Excitement mounting, I rang the ironmongers in Egham and said that I wanted some painting equipment.

"What do you want to paint?" asked a voice, patiently.

"A cathedral," I said. "At night. In a gale."

About an hour later a van backed up the drive and two men unloaded eight twenty-gallon drums of Exterior Brown and Exterior

Black, a long ladder and a powerful torch. Also a collection of six-inch brushes and a set of oilskins.

I put on the oilskins, opened a drum of paint, stirred it with the torch and got cracking. It was surprising how short a time it took to paint an oil painting when I was using a six-inch brush. It was finished within the hour. I painted the dome in the pinky-brown paint and painted the sky black to show it was night. I then dabbed in the windows with some red paint I found in the garage and flicked some black here and there to give the illusion of a storm. I then strode away some ten feet, turned and had a good look at what I had got. It gave me quite a turn. It did not look like the Duomo in Florence at all. The dome looked for all the world like the head of a braw Scots laddie. The windows looked like his bloodshot eyes, the two smaller domes became his ears, the little spire in front was his nose and the great lantern on top of the dome just came out as a huge lump on his head. It was a bitterly disappointing moment.

What to do about it?

I decided to accept the inevitable and with a small sigh and a rag soaked in turpentine I wiped off the title 'Florence: Night in Gale' and painted in 'The Laddie with the Lump'.

The picture was never exhibited, of course. Not only was the subject wrong but just after I had finished painting it I swung the up-and-over garage door up to get the car out and the top of the frame scraped all the paint off the tarpaulin.

It was only later that night, as I lay sleepless in bed wondering what to do with the remaining hundred and fifty-nine and a half gallons of Exterior Paint, that the great thought dawned: how many of the world's great works of art had, like 'The Laddie with the Lump', started out as something else entirely? How many of our masterpieces are, in fact, only masterpieces because of some accident?

If my theory was true it would revolutionise all our concepts of genius and the creative spirit. Anybody could have a go as long as they were either accident-prone or lucky.

The following morning, even though it was spitting with rain, I made my way to the Virginia Water Public Library and flung myself into research.

I reached down a book of Leonardo da Vinci's work and sat for an hour staring at a reproduction of 'Mona Lisa'. How had that picture started out, I asked myself? What was the real story that lay behind such an odd portrait? Suddenly the picture spoke out to me and yielded up its secret. Quite clearly Leonardo had set out to paint a picture entitled 'Model With a Slightly Green Face Spitting Water Through her Front Teeth'. He had found a model in the cabarets of Florence, a slightly green-faced singer named Lisa Minelli, and began painting furiously. But Lisa did not take well to modelling and complained loudly throughout the sittings; "Why you paint-a like thees all day? Is no work for a man. Is sissy-work. Why you no getta job like a real Italiano. Be a waiter. I waste-a my time 'ere. I could-a be at 'ome enjoying my tagliatelli (Italian television)."

And so destiny took a hand and when the portrait was finished Leonardo decided not to call it 'Model With a Slightly Green Face Spitting Water Through her Front Teeth' – a hopeless title which would have doomed the picture to oblivion – and called it instead 'Moaner Lisa' ('Mona' in Italian) thus winning himself immortality and half a yard on the wall of the Louvre.

I then moved to sculpture. Rodin's famous statue of the embracing couple entitled 'The Kiss'. The more I stared at a picture of it the more I became convinced that Rodin had not set out to sculpt what he ended up with. No, I am of the firm opinion that Rodin began by sculpting two quite separate statues, one male and one female, in crouching positions with arms outstretched and bent, perhaps entitled 'Male and Female Nudes About to begin their Friday Evening Kung-Fu Exercises'. But when they were finished he loaded them into the back of a lorry and in his anxiety to get them swiftly to the Exhibition Hall rounded the Place de la Concorde in a tight turn and the two statues crashed together, became interlocked, and have stayed that way ever since.

Franz Hals' 'The Laughing Cavalier'? Originally painted clean-shaven? Would he have been exhibited clean-shaven had not Hals left the painting leaning up against the wall of the Underground station while he bought his ticket?

But the most striking example of my theory in action is my hypothesis of the creation of 'The Angelus' by the French painter Jean Millet. How on earth, I asked myself, did this drab masterpiece of two peasants leaning on their hoes come to be painted by the vivacious young artist who was even then known to his friends as Thoroughly Modern Millet?

84

My theory runs thus. Millet was on a walking tour with his two friends Toulouse-Lautrec and Karl Marx when he saw these two peasants, clad in toil-worn French peasant-type blue jeans, leaning on their hoes while the distant church rang the Angelus.

"What a great idea for a masterpiece!" he exclaims boyishly. "Quick, my palette and plenty of paint, mainly Exterior Brown and Blue!" He rapidly begins to set up his portable easel.

"Un moment, mon brave," says Toulouse-Lautrec. "Not so vite. I have a better idea. Get the peasants to change into their best party clothes and paint a picture of them doing the Can-Can. That's what the Salon likes these days, frills, frou-frous and leg!"

"Right," says Millet. "You heard what Toulouse said, Karl. Would you mind asking the peasants to change into evening dress for me?"

Off goes Karl Marx. Chats with the peasants. Returns, face glum.

"No go, I'm afraid," he says. "They have nothing to change into." And then he adds the line which has gone into the history books and which gave Millet his masterpiece:

"The workers have nothing, Toulouse, but their jeans."

I think, therefore I am

René Descartes

ALTHOUGH that line launched René Descartes on his meteoric rise to stardom, what he actually wrote was something slightly different. So I can't tell you the pleasure it now gives me to put the record straight, if only for his sake.

I say that because life was not all roses for this seventeenth-century philosopher. In the first place, he'd been saddled with that unfortunate Christian name, and even though the French pronounce it 'Renay' it was still one hell of a liability for a growing lad in those rough times. Secondly, when he came to manhood he married this real granite-block of a wife. Although Mme Descartes brought some property to the marriage, the truth is she was several years his senior, had the disposition of an untipped taxi-driver and was an inveterate picture-straightener. Every time Descartes sat down to work on a crystalline aphorism in she'd come, still in her rollers, with – "I'm sorry, but I need this room for a social gathering." Or – "If you don't mind, kindly shift your philosophy kit to the shed."

It is hard to think of a way in which she could have been other than a millstone to any aspiring philosopher. Even in their more intimate moments, when he managed to steel himself for an attempt at love-making, her invariable response was the phrase which Gershwin was later to put to such melodious use – "Descartes, take that away from me."

You may wonder then, how was it, in such an unpromising work-environment, that René still managed to make Number One among philosophy's all-time chart-toppers? Well, as I've indicated, it's all down to the widespread misunderstanding about his line 'I think, therefore I am'. And to trace the *exact* origin of that I must take you back to the New Year's Eve party which Madame Descartes threw to celebrate the advent of 1636.

As it was to be an informal affair, she'd decided to serve the guests 'buffet-style', which is a French expression meaning 'we've got more people than chairs'. As she also intended it to be a late do, with no one even arriving till around 11 p.m., she ran up an enormous bunch of that Gallic imitation of bacon-and-egg flan they call *quiches*. Not the large family-sized ones, but those small individual versions so affectionately celebrated by Yvette Guilbert. ('Just a leetle love, a leetle quiche.')

However – and you'll be glad to know we're now getting somewhere near the point of all this – Madame made it clear to René that although the quiches were all to be put out on the sideboard beforehand – "the one thing I *don't* want to see is people helping themselves in advance and treading their crumbs into the Aubusson. So I'm relying on you to see that nobody starts digging into them until at least one hour after we've seen the New Year in. Then they can take plates and eat properly."

Ironic, isn't it? The founder of the Cartesian school of philosophy relegated to the position of Securicor for bacon-and-egg flans. As he himself said to Father Dinet – I haven't mentioned him before, but he was the Jesuit priest who was just about the only real mate René had at that time – as he said to him "I can't think this is in any way advancing my career. Being sat down here at the sideboard till one o'clock in the morning, that's no way to get any philosophising done tomorrow, I'll be like a limp rag."

To which the good Father rejoined an extremely practical rejoinder. "Well, why don't you use *this* as working-time? Take a writing-instrument and, while you're sitting here, set your mind for lofty thoughts. Then, if any crop up, jot them down on a paper serviette."

"Nice thinking," said Descartes. "Give us a borrow of your quill then."

It worked extremely well. For the next hour or so the two friends sat quietly by the sideboard and Descartes was able to get off quite a few zingers relating to corporeal rationality. It was while he was fashioning an eternal verity on adventitious volition that he glanced up and, to his horror, saw what had happened. Father

Dinet had helped himself to a quiche and was absently munching it.

. Just as Descartes was about to exclaim, "Watch it, mate, they're not supposed to be eaten yet," he became aware of something else. There, well within earshot, stood his wife! There was only one thing to do. Stealthily, Descartes took another serviette, scribbled his warning on it, then – equally furtively – pushed the serviette under the priest's nose.

Thus it was that the whole three-hundred-year-old misunderstanding originated. That message, the one which Father Dinet was later to publish to the world as 'I think, therefore I am', was in fact only a reference to the time-ban on the bacon-and-egg flans.

All it actually said was:

'I think they're for 1 a.m.'

'A Policeman's Lot is Not a Happy One'

W. S. Gilbert
Song from 'The Pirates of Penzance'

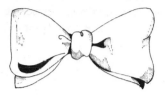

THE phone rang.

"Good morning," said the editor of my local paper *The Staines and Egham News*, "I badly need your help."

I had been waiting for just such a call for some years. It seemed incredible to me that the newspaper had not called upon my talents before to boost its circulation.

"It is yours to command," I riposted firmly. "I have in mind a satirical, hard-hitting yet compassionate column ripping the lid off the inefficiency and downright indifference of local council . . ."

I thought I detected a sigh at the other end of the phone.

"No," he said. "Could you take over our 'Advice to the Lovelorn' column just for this week? Estelle Laverne is indisposed."

"Nothing serious I trust?"

"Just routine. He drank too much after playing rugger and got his beard caught in the pub's glass-washing machine. I will bung on the letters as they come in."

I agreed. He bunged.

Hardly had I got over my sickening disappointment at finding that Estelle Laverne was a bearded, rugger-playing male – I had always enjoyed her lambent prose-style; she was particularly sensitive in advising schoolgirls embarrassed by enormous busts, and happily-married solicitors who fancied the lady Parking-Meter Attendant – when I was further disappointed. Only one Lovelorn reader wrote in for Advice.

I shall call him Lafcadio Quilp to protect his anonymity, though that is not his real name (his mother is the dreadful Mrs Snaith who ruins the school dinners at a Staines educational establishment. I have met her son Ron a few times. A deeply thick lad. It surprised me that he was able to write his name let alone a request for Advice).

Ron's – that is to say Lafcadio's – problem was a simple one. Whilst skate-boarding to work along Thorpe Green Road he had glimpsed and become enamoured of the daughter of our new village constable. He had managed to find out her name, which was Lottie Leatherbarrow. Should he take his chance in the lottery of life or should he first make enquiries and ensure that Lottie Leatherbarrow was kind in thought, word and deed and not a sharp-tongued, nagging harpy like his own dear mother?

My duty as the surrogate Estelle Laverne was clear. I must make discreet enquiries myself about Miss Leatherbarrow. Engage her in light banter. Observe how she reacted under pressure. I would then be in a strong position to give Ron Snaith the advice he sought.

As it happened I was distracted from doing anything further by a number of small domestic issues which engaged my time over the next few weeks, principally the choice of a Fancy-Dress costume to wear at a Ball in Norfolk I had agreed to attend. In the event it was a double function – my first and my last Fancy-Dress Ball. I will not weary you with details of the humiliations I suffered day after day as the staff of Nathans Theatrical Costumiers tried to stuff my bent six-feet-five frame into costumes which ranged from The Artful Dodger to Harlequin. Eventually, haggard, they flung an old red Father-Christmas cloak round me, thrust my head up through a paper doiley and said "That's it. Cardinal Richelieu!"

I did not enjoy the Ball.

And I did not enjoy the trip home. Something went wrong with the gear-box on my car and I had to do the whole journey in first gear, max speed 15 mph. Dawn broke round about Watford and it was nine o'clock on the Sunday morning when the car, which had been giving off steam like a kettle for miles, coughed, twanged and expired within sight of the transport café on the A.4 near Ascot.

"Good-morning, Father," said the café proprietor reverently as I went up to the counter. "And what would you be after having?"

I pulled my red robes closer against the cold of the morning.

"I need a lift," I said. "To Thorpe."

"Ah," he said, "It's lucky you are this morning, that it is, it is that. Those two lads there are doing overtime on the M.25 extension at Thorpe and it is there that they will be going, that they will, oh yes, Father."

And so it proved. But the vehicle they were driving was not entirely suitable for hitch-hikers. It was an hydraulic crane used for messing about with the motorway lamp-standards. It had a little cabin stuck onto a couple of hinged girders. When the driver pulled a lever the cabin rose up to the required height and whoever was crouched within the little cabin could get on with his work. As the inside of the vehicle was wholly occupied by the two lads, an enormous collie dog and a baby in a pram I had to grit my teeth and squat in the little cabin outside. But it was summer and not too windy and we bowled along happily.

It was as we were going along Thorpe Green that I suddenly realised that we were coming up to our village constable's house. The memory of my duty to Ron Snaith flooded back. The driver had given me the code they used – one thump on the floor to start the vehicle, two thumps to stop it. I thumped twice. The crane stopped.

"Yes?"

"Can you raise me so that I am level with that bedroom window there? There's somebody inside I have to talk to."

"Right."

The driver must have pulled a lever because my little cabin and I rose swiftly until we were level with the window and then moved forward until I was right up against the sill.

It was Lottie's bedroom, happily. And Lottie was combing her hair at her dressing-table. She seemed surprised to see me but opened the window affably.

"I speak on behalf of Ron Snaith," I said. "Could you join me in my little cabin for a minute. I want to engage you in banter and see how you react under pressure."

It was a bit of a shock when she climbed over the sill because she was wearing a very short nighty which appeared to be almost totally transparent. And her figure I can only describe as effeminate.

"Who is Ron Snaith?" she was about to say when she stumbled and fell with a thump on the floor of the cabin.

Taking this as the code signal the driver put the lorry into gear and roared away. Trying to help Lottie to her feet without actually looking at her or touching her I managed to thump twice on the floor and the crane came to a stop again.

"Take us back!" I shouted downwards. "Get us back, lads, please!"

"Right," came the reply. "We'll back up."

"We'd better kneel down," I said to Lottie, "Less chance of being seen."

The lorry backed and weaved and we in the cabin went up and down a few times and then came to rest against a window.

"Wait a minute," said Lottie suddenly, "This isn't my house!"

But it was too late. The window was flung up and glaring out in disbelief at us was the unlovely face of Mrs Gooch, village gossip, defender of morals and scourge of the wicked.

"What," she muttered between clenched teeth, "is the meaning of this?"

I knelt there, frozen with fear. I could see the headlines in the *Staines and Egham News*: 'SEX SCANDAL SHOCK HORROR REVELATION. FAKE CARDINAL AND POLICEMAN'S DAUGHTER CAUGHT IN CRANE'. I glanced fearfully at Lottie. Would she tear into the woman and give the old trout a piece of her mind, thus dooming us?

"Oh really," said Lottie, eyes modestly cast down. "Can't a girl go to mobile confessional on a Sunday morning?"

I can now state a fact:

Our policeman's Lottie's not a harpy, Ron.

Splendour in the grass

William Wordsworth
'Intimations of Immortality'

FIELD Marshals, Admirals Of The Fleet, Air Vice Marshals and other distinguished members of the Imperial Staff College. . . . While feeling extremely honoured at being asked to deliver this year's Kilroy Lecture, I must admit to some surprise at receiving the invitation; if only because the last time I was summoned to the presence of so many high-ranking officers was during the D-Day Landings when General Montgomery fell into a latrine-trench I had dug.

That sharply-etched memory, however, only spurred my determination to find a subject suitable to this annual lecture whose theme, by tradition, is always 'a neglected feat of military heroism'. To that end, I set myself the task of reading through the entire contents of my local library's 'Military History' section. If that turned out a less onerous undertaking than I'd feared, it was because all the shelf contained was a copy of *The Wooden Horse* and a bound volume of Vera Lynn hits.

Happily, though, the first of these – Mr Williams' excellent escape-story – did suggest to me an episode suitable to this occasion. Accordingly, the neglected feat of military heroism I would now like to recall is the one that took place inside that original and prototype Wooden Horse: the legendary decoy by which the Greeks gained final victory in their altercation with the Trojans. While this ingenious instrument-of-war has itself been frequently acclaimed in song and story, those to whom no tribute has ever been paid are the platoon of humble Greek soldiers whose duty it was to sit inside it for three days. Let me therefore, by drawing on memories of my own Service experiences as an L.A.C.,

93

endeavour to reconstruct their agonising ordeal.

It is likely to have begun, as all my agonising military ordeals began, with a briefing from a non-commissioned officer. Probably, I would venture, a sergeant with two long-service stripes.

"All right now, settle down and hold the jaw, let's have some quiet. And quiet means QUIET. That's better. Well now, you've probably all been wondering what this huge wooden thing under the dust-sheets might be when it's at home. All right then, you are now going to be given the privilege of I'm showing you. Corporal, whip off them dust-sheets. . . . There you are, men. What about that then?"

"What is it, Sarge?"

"What do you mean 'What is it, Sarge?' Trust you, Epidoros, to ask what is it. If you wore your helmet on straight, my lad, you'd see what it is. It's an horse. That's what it is. A enormous dirty great wooden horse. And we're calling it The Horse Of Troy."

"You mean like the Mare of Blackpool?"

"No, I do not mean like the Mare of Blackpool, Epidoros. I mean it is an siege-breaking weapon what is going to be filled with something. And do you know what it is going to be filled with, Epidoros?"

". . . Toffees?"

"Toffees. Oh you disgust me sometimes, Epidoros. You really do. Great gormless Greek! How can toffees be used for siege-breaking purposes? No, what that horse is going to be filled with, me lucky lads, is you. All of you. Right then. On the command 'Enter Horse' I want to see this platoon file smartly inside the beast in Alpha Beta order. Entah – HOWSSE!"

"Through where, Sarge?"

"What do you mean, 'Through where'?"

"Where do we enter it? Do we go in through the mouth?"

"Course you do not go in through the mouth! Ordinary eighteen-pence should tell you you cannot enter an horse through the mouth!"

"Well, where then? . . . Hey, you're not getting me to –"

"Through the *trapdoor*! The special trapdoor what has been cut through its midriff! And one more word out of you, Epidoros, I'll have you up in front of the Colonel before you can say Agope-mone!"

That then, gentlemen, was the start of their ordeal. What lay ahead was even worse. Try and imagine the torment it must have been for twenty men to sit, shoulder-to-shoulder, inside the confines of a wooden equine facsimile for three endless days.

"Sarge. . . ."

"Sh!"

"*Sarge!*"

"Will you keep your voice down! Want the bleeding Trojans to tumble us?"

"But it's Epidoros, Sarge."

"What about Epidoros?"

"He's got one of his tummies."

"Oh no. No! Not in *here*! Hang on, Epidoros! Attention everybody – can I have your attention, please? . . . Is there a doctor in the horse?"

Picture it, gentlemen. Discomfort, heat, hunger, thirst, enforced silence, no ablution facilities, no Naafi lady. But even those privations pale into insignificance beside the worst torture that gallant little band found itself subjected to. . . .

What every historian has neglected to take into account is that they were all citizens of Greece. In other words, the uniform they were wearing was that of the Greek Army. And we all know what that consists of – a short, flimsy *skirt*! Now, when you couple that skirt with the fact that the seats on which they were obliged to sit were of *wooden* construction – well, need I say more? If you can imagine your own practically bare hindquarters shifting about on rough, unpolished wood for a span of seventy-two hours – then, gentlemen, your personal and ever-present agony is not going to be Wordsworth's 'splendour in the *grass*' is it?

What it's much more likely to be is '*splinter* in . . . gentlemen-I-thank-you-for-your-attention'.

Chacun à son goût

French proverb

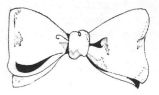

'Each to his own taste' say the French and for once I agree with them. The French have quite a few philosophical sayings based on food, e.g. 'Sôle Bonne Femme et un oeuf' ('One good woman is enough'), 'Tarte à la Maison' ('The girl lives here'), 'Sauce Tartare' ('Bye-bye, Cheeky!'), but I am inclined to disbelieve most of them. It seems to me that the French nation has conned the rest of the world over a period of centuries into believing that only the French know how to cook food.

My own taste is for British food, cooked in the traditional British way. I speak of lunch, the only meal which I cook for myself. When my wife is out I drag myself away from the typewriter for exactly thirty minutes. During that time I prepare and consume a nicely balanced meal which sets me up for the afternoon's labours.

Until recently my nicely balanced lunch was the same every day: an inch and a half of cheddar and a banana.

Then I became more ambitious. I started to read some cookery book or other. The title escapes me. Was it something by John le Carrier called *The Pie Who Came in from the Cold*? No matter. The important thing is that it gave a recipe for what it called A Simple British Cooked Lunch. None of your Frenchified rubbish, you notice. Good plain food, simply cooked.

'Use butter for frying', said the recipe. I got a pound of butter out of the fridge, unwrapped it and slid it into a frying-pan.

'Melt the butter', said the recipe. I lit the gas and turned it full on. After about ten minutes an element of drama crept into the proceedings. The kitchen filled with smoke of a most subtle and

96

delicate blue colour and about a quart of hot fluid bubbled away cheerfully in the pan.

'Now insert your rasher of bacon', said the recipe. It was a bit tricky getting near enough to the pan what with the smoke and the heat but I managed to lob the rasher into the pan at the third attempt and stood by to turn it when done.

Then a most extraordinary phenomenon occurred. The hot butter began spitting like an hysterical cat and there seemed to be about two hundred tiny, invisible wasps stinging the backs of my hands and my forehead.

I retreated behind the door and appraised the situation coolly. It was clear that the spitting hot fat had an effective range of about five feet. If the rasher of bacon was to be turned, as per instructions, then I either had to turn it from six feet away with the aid of a long-handled tool like a garden rake, or protect myself from the wasps by hiding behind some sort of a shield.

The garden rake was useless. Its teeth were too far apart to pick up the bacon and all I succeeded in doing was splashing hot fat up the kitchen wall. The fork used for dung-spreading was a little better because its tines were sharp. I managed to spear the bacon after the fourth stab but in trying to turn it I dropped it down behind the fridge. While I was scooping it out with the rake and holding it under the tap to wash off some of the debris I came to the decision that a shield would be better.

And it was. For those of my readers about to venture into cooking A Simple British Cooked Lunch for the first time I have the perfect answer to the spitting fat problem. Borrow, hire or buy a motor-scooter. These vehicles have a huge, transparent plastic shield fitted on them to stop the rider being lacerated by rain. Wheel the scooter into the kitchen and park it facing the frying-pan, some three feet away. Crouch behind the screen. You will be protected from the flying fat yet be able to see the state of play of the bacon. Over your right arm you will have slipped a two-foot length of six-inch drainage pipe and a stout gardening-glove. When the bacon is due to be turned you merely reach round the screen with your armoured arm and turn the rasher by hand.

I got out two eggs, put them on the top of the refrigerator and consulted the cookery book. 'Now fry your eggs', the book said. I turned to the refrigerator and the eggs had disappeared. I got out two more and put them on the refrigerator. As I watched they gave

97

a little shudder and, lemming-like, waddled over to the edge and committed suicide, joining their two shattered brothers on the floor below.

I got out two more eggs and rested them on the draining-board of the sink reckoning that the grooves in the draining-board would stop the eggs from rolling off. This they did satisfactorily but failed to stop the eggs from rolling *down*. In fact, as the draining-board sloped towards the sink the eggs fairly hurtled down.

I resolved to hold eggs numbers seven and eight in my hand and take advice as to my next move. The cookery book recommended cracking the eggs by tapping them gently against a sharp edge, such as the lip of a saucepan. I got out a saucepan and did as instructed. Half the shell fell into the saucepan and the other half – plus the egg – fell to the floor. I had better luck with the other egg. I managed to get half the egg as well as half the shell into the saucepan. I went back to the cookery book.

'Another method of cracking eggs,' it said, 'is to crack the shell lightly, urge both thumbs into the crack and pull steadily apart – this will enable the egg yolk to drop out undamaged.' Give credit where it is due. This method worked superly although, looking back, I think I should have cracked the egg over a pan.

With eggs numbers ten and eleven I devised my own method which worked well and I have used it ever since. You simply stand over a receptacle with the egg held firmly in your hand and squeeze. The runny stuff, which is not all that runny, seeps between your fingers and the shell is retained. Or some of it is.

I cannot recall ever having enjoyed a meal as much as I enjoyed that Simple British Cooked Lunch.

The bacon was like no other I had ever eaten. It was a unique culinary sensation. Tiny, like a fragile, twisted, dead oak-leaf, it tasted like a fragment of salty charcoal.

And the fried eggs, though they looked a little like a pair of buttons clad in frilly black lace petticoats, were tender and sliced easily with the help of a serrated carving-knife.

Such a meal of good, honest ingredients and traditional cooking methods is quite beyond the French, of course. They must always overdo everything, like pouring liqueur over the food and setting fire to it.

I had a go at cooking à la française once and believe me it just does not work. At the back of my cookery book it gave a recipe for a typically French bit of 'haute cuisine' (which I always thought meant 'how to cook porridge'). The recipe required me to make a thin omelet, chuck half a pint of brandy over it while it was still hot and 'flambé' it, i.e. set it on fire.

My omelet turned out quite well. I used eighteen eggs – my aim wasn't too good that evening – and we were out of brandy so I chucked on half a litre of methylated spirits and lit it. Well! The French may like to cook like that but it is hardly to the British taste. As the match touched the meths there was a loud 'whooosh', a sheet of flame leaped up and set the kitchen curtains on fire and the omelet turned into a wet, soggy mess.

So as far as I am concerned the French taste for 'haute cuisine' can be summed up in an old English proverbial phrase which I have just made up:

Chuck on . . . arson . . . goo.

'Where the Blue of the Night Meets the Gold of the Day'

Popular song
Fred E. Ahler, Roy Turk and Bing Crosby

LAST July, about half-past eleven one morning, I received a telephone-call from my wife. "Do not, on any account, have a big lunch today."

"Why not?"

"Because for dinner tonight I'm cooking you a leg of lamb, roast chicken, veal cutlets, braised tongue, shepherd's pie and meat loaf."

I said, "I'll never eat all that lot."

"You'd better try," she said. "The deep-freeze has gone wrong."

Even before the 'ong' in her 'wrong' had died away, I was on the other line to our local service-engineer, a chap we used to call 'that little man in the electrical shop' but who's nowadays referred to as 'the gentleman who owns that big house with two Aston Martins in the drive'. When he came to the phone, I hailed him by the friendly nickname by which he prefers us to address him, "Sir," I said. "Our deep-freeze is on the blink."

"Must be a short-circuit," he said.

"In that case, sir," I said, "Could you possibly come over and lengthen it?"

He gave one of those deep satisfied chuckles you only hear from a technical person who's just confirmed he's talking to a mug. "Be round within the month."

When the bill for his services arrived, I glanced at its total and without a word of a lie I thought it was an offer for the house. After I'd cancelled our summer holiday and paid it, I made a solemn vow. The next time any kind of domestic electrical fault developed, I would repair it myself.

There are two grounds on which that pledge could be considered foolhardy. The first is that where anything to do with electrical matters is concerned I work from a basis of almost Neanderthal ignorance. (Asked by small son how it is that the same electricity which makes the deep-freeze cold is also able to make the toaster hot, I explained it's because the toaster is on the opposite side of the kitchen.) The second is that whenever you permit yourself to make an avowal of that kind, fate always takes you up on it.

Sure enough, little more than a week later, I arrived home to find that something had gone amiss with the interior illumination of our refrigerator. When you opened the fridge door, instead of that little light coming on and floodlighting the food on display, it was all sort of dark and crepuscular in there, which is not only inconvenient but it doesn't half make a two-day-old pizza look cruddy. Well, as technical problems go, it was a challenging one but now and again I do get these delusions of adequacy so I borrowed the screwdriver from small son's laser-beam kit and set to. The first problem was, I couldn't even find where the light-source was located. After searching the entire interior from yoghurts to orange juice, I admitted myself defeated and decided to tackle the job a different way.

Instead of repairing that light-source I would fit an entirely new one. By installing an ordinary twenty-five-watt bulb under the compartment that holds the ice-trays, not only would it give all the illumination necessary but if I also covered the bulb with one of those red-velvet lamp-shades, the whole interior of the fridge would look downright sexy.

I gained an enormous sense of satisfaction when it all worked out as I'd planned, especially as the entire job took no longer than three hours. Mind you, when I say three hours, I suppose it was nearer eleven really, if you count the periods when I had to come out of the fridge to thaw. Well, it had been decided I'd better work squatting inside it with the door closed, because of the three pieces of haddock we were keeping for Tuesday. You know how quickly haddock goes off if the fridge door's left open. Even at that, my candle frizzled the edges of the two bacon rashers for Wednesday. But, that apart – and discounting the fact that my overcoat and woolly gloves still niff slightly of haddock – all that aside, my new interior light works every bit as well as the former one and the fridge is as good as ever.

Well no. To be completely honest, not quite as good as ever. Screwing that light-bulb under the ice-tray compartment did have one side-effect. The ice-cubes are not really as cold as they were. As a matter of fact, they're inclined to be rather warm. Well, to come right out with it, our ice-cubes *boil*.

Now, I suppose all you electrical experts out there have already twigged the technical reason for it. I say that because, when I rang Sir to ask where all this unprecedented heat could be coming from, the phrase he used to indicate its location seemed a fairly familiar one:

Where the screw of the light meets the cold of the tray.

One penny plain and twopence coloured

Robert Louis Stevenson
'Travels With a Donkey'

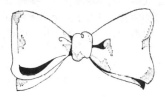

BUT for that one fatal slip I might have got away with it. As it is I have no recourse but to face the full majesty of the law and pay my debt to society.

The events which led to my downfall, I now see, followed one upon the other inexorably, with the inevitability of Greek tragedy, beginning when I tried to drag the cat down from a kitchen cupboard and tipped a two-pound jar of home-made marmalade over my wife.

There is a surprising quantity of marmalade in a two-pound jar. Sticky dollops of the stuff shot all over the place, up the wall, under the refrigerator, across the cooker, but most of it landed on my wife's head. And we had no shampoo in the house.

Accepting that I was partly to blame for what had happened I volunteered to drive to a shop and buy shampoo.

"With Lanolin," said my wife. "Any shampoo as long as it contains Lanolin."

"Lanolin?" I replied, puzzled. "Where does that come from?"

"It comes from Wool. Everybody knows that lanolin comes from Wool."

"Then from Wool it shall come!" I retorted assuringly, grabbing the AA *Book of the Road* and making for the car.

Wool turned out to be a small town, or large village, in Dorset, about half-way between Bournemouth and Weymouth, and a fine old drive from Thorpe, Surrey. It was dark by the time I arrived at Wool but I found a shop open and bought a shampoo guaranteed by the proprietor, hand on heart, to contain lanolin.

Things began to go awry from then on. I picked up a hitchhiker, a student, who told me all about the trouble with his girl-friend. It seems that she had taken up a form of Yoga which resulted in her spending most evenings upside down on the carpet resting upon her head. His objections to this were not on religious or moral but aesthetic grounds. Apparently she lost her looks when reversed. Her bottom and bust assumed gross proportions like, he said, a primitive wood-carving, and her eyes became malevolent. I persuaded him to start anew with her. To adopt an inverted pos-ture on the carpet next to her whereupon she should once again appear normal in his eyes. He thanked me warmly and persuaded me to drive him home to Birmingham.

It was four o'clock in the morning when I found myself in Lyne Lane, only a mile from home but the fog thickening. I don't know whether you know Lyne Lane but I usually only approach it from the Thorpe direction and I know full well that there is the Runny-mede Council Rubbish tip on the right and the sewage disposal plant on the left. I decided to check my position in the fog by get-ting out of the car and locating with my hands the huge chain-link gates of the rubbish tip. But I had forgotten that I was facing the other way. I walked through the fog searching with my hands for the gates but could not find them. I walked on and on and event-ually fell into a pit of something. I was soaked through, head to foot, in the something and it stank to high heaven.

It was clear that I could not go home in that condition, wet, reeking and totally unacceptable socially. But what could be done about it? Ah. I remembered that Virginia Water, but a mile up the road, had in its esplanade of shops a 24-hour, coin-operated dry-cleaners. I got back in the car and crept gently to Virginia Water. Yes, there was the dry-cleaners, lights a-blaze, empty.

In a flash I nipped into the shop, switched the lights out, stripped naked, stuffed everything into the machine, banged the door shut, thumbed in the appropriate coins and sat down to wait.

It then occurred to me that my car headlights were full on out-side, just asking for the police, or some busybody, to investigate what was going on.

Like a shadow I crept out of the door, switched my lights off and went back to the shop. But the door would not open. From force of habit I had slipped the catch on leaving and had now locked myself out.

A car suddenly came through the fog, headlights on. I crouched in a heap, making a sound like a small hawthorn bush, and watched the car stop at the far end of the row of shops.

I considered my position. My chances of driving home unobserved, stark naked, were slim. My best plan would be to find somewhere warm to spend the hours until daylight and then formulate a plan to retrieve my clothes from the dry-cleaners.

The car that went past! Yes, of course, it was the baker going on duty at the bakery, the last shop on the esplanade. Bakers always begin work before dawn.

I made my way stealthily through the night past the dead shop-fronts. Yes, the bakery was lit up. The door was unlocked. I slipped into the warmth and hid beneath a shelf of unsold assorted French pastries.

". . . ooooh give ME that night divine, let my arms INto yours entwine . . ." sang the baker, switching on this and that, and banging about in the bakery behind the shop. I heard his footsteps approaching and pressed my bare body into a rack of meringues.

". . . the Desert Song is caLLING . . ." he sang, switching out the lights, and exiting, locking the shop door behind him.

I reconsidered my position. I was locked in but I was at least locked into somewhere most agreeably warm. I had no clothes on. The baker had presumably lit his oven and was returning home for breakfast or a cup of tea or something while it heated up. There was every chance that he would return within half an hour when, if I could find some sort of clothing, I could make my escape.

I looked about me. Hanging up behind the door were some pinafores which the ladies who served in the shop wore. They were plain blue. The same as worn by the girls who bashed the tills at the supermarket four doors up. A plan began to form in my head. If I put on one of the plain pinnies and scraped my hair into a bouffant style I could make a dash for my car and, if stopped, pretend to be a girl-cashier who had worked late. I tried on a pinny. It fitted fairly well except that it did not meet at the back, which was worrying. I pulled my hair forward and messed it about to make it look feminine. I dipped a finger into a raspberry tartlet and reddened my lips. But there was still something wrong. Of course! My figure! Happily the fog was beginning to clear and a fitful moon gave enough light for me to see the shelves. I selected a pair of sticky buns; large buns covered with sticky stuff of a particularly revolting pink colour. Holding them pink sticky stuff inwards I rammed them against my chest. They adhered. I then pulled my plain blue pinny over them and I had the indications of femininity that I needed. Well satisfied, I curled up beneath the counter for a short rest before the baker returned.

Perhaps it was the long drive to Wool and back via Birmingham, perhaps the warmth of the bakery, but when I awoke it was twelve o'clock on Saturday morning and the shop was full of ladies buying bread.

It was one of the nastiest moments of my life but I did not panic. I resolved to make a dash for it. I got to my feet.

"Must get back to my till," I lisped, and minced out through the gaping ladies, clutching the fissure at the back where the pinny did not meet. Once outside I broke into a shambling trot, dived into my car and drove home, confident that I had got away with it.

But I had made one fatal slip. I had broken the law of the land in making my escape from the bakery and must answer to the magistrates' court for the offence, which is, according to the summons – that I did steal, appropriate, or convert to my own use property belonging to the Virginia Water Bakery as under:

One pinny – plain, and two buns – coloured.

A triumph of mind over matter

G. Paley
Natural Theology, 1819

I T'S always a saddening moment, unexpectedly meeting one of your boyhood sweethearts again. But to run across her in Soho, leaning boldly against a lamp-post –! That was heart-wrenching. The funny thing was, I recognised her immediately. A sudden coldness clutching at my heart, I said, "It's – it's Sandy, isn't it?"

"Isn't what, darling?"

"Your name." Then I remembered it wasn't. Her real name was Muriel. Sandy was only what I used to call her, because of the colour of her hair. In those days it was all golden and sparkling, like Sugar Frosties on a clear morning.

She stared at me without interest. Then her expression changed. "Stone me," she whispered. "Soppy."

That had been her pet-name for me; coined, I think, because my other pre-occupation at that time was constructing models of Sopwith aircraft. But just hearing her utter the word brought that whole portion of my life back again. The summer of '38 . . . Munich, Little Audrey jokes, trolley-buses, The Lambeth Walk, Joan Crawford and Clark Gable in *Forsaking All Others*. (Yes, I know that went out on General Release in 1934, but it didn't reach Stamford Hill till 1938.) And, through all those troubled days, Sandy and I roaming the windswept uplands of Clissold Park together, little fingers linked, an arm around each other's shoulders, sharing between us an Eldorado choc-ice. No easy task, I remembered ruefully, when neither of you has a hand free.

"Oh, Sandy," I said. "Do you ever think about – the Curiously Strong Peppermints?" A flicker crossed her face. Curiously Strong

Peppermints had been another of our 'shared' things. They dated from an evening in her father's air-raid shelter when she whispered "I'm narf cold" and moved closer to me. It was an invitation to which I responded with that surge of physical impulse only youth can muster. Jumping on my Raleigh, I pedalled full-pelt to the sweet-shop and brought her back a tin of those mints. Thereafter we never went anywhere without them and it was also from that evening she took to addressing me by that pet-name.

As I looked at her now, something within me ached at what the years do to us. Time had treated her looks kindly enough – her hair shone with the same golden hue I remembered and the shiny black stockings she wore still disturbed my senses – but my soul raged at the cruel fate that had reduced her to her present circumstances. Walking the streets!

"Oh, Sandy," I found myself saying. "What was it? What forced you into this kind of life?"

She shrugged. "The money."

"But to let yourself become a – a . . ." I swallowed, shook my head.

"A what?" she said, tauntingly. "Can't even say the word? You haven't changed much, Soppy."

Her mockery stung me. "All right, I will say it. Did you have to become a Traffic Warden?"

Her eyes blazed. "If it wasn't for men like you," she said, "there would be no need for women like me."

"Sandy," I said. "Listen to me. For old time's sake, won't you let me take you away from –" I gestured helplessly "– this?"

"This what?"

"This BMW. It's mine. And I'm only four minutes over the time. Please," I implored, "for the sake of what we once had together, couldn't you just wander up the road a bit further? Only for a minute or so. Just long enough for me to shove another 5p in."

Stubbornly, she shook her head. Despite my anguish, I could recognise the irony of the situation. What a world it's become when a man finds himself pleading with a woman because *he's* overdue! My mind was churning like a tumble-dryer. Then suddenly, it calmed. I knew what I had to do. "Look, Sandy," I said. "Look, my dear." And from the recesses of my executive shoulder-bag I drew forth a tin of Curiously Strong Peppermints.

I have never seen female features soften so instantly. I think I

108

even detected a glint of moisture in her eyes. "You – you still carry them?" she faltered. "Still?"

"Everywhere," I said. "And I think I always will."

Those even white teeth clamped down on her lower lip. With a broken word I didn't quite catch, she turned on her smartly-polished heel and strode off towards Shaftesbury Avenue.

And that's all there was to the reunion except, as always, for the things that were left unsaid. In this case, I have to confess they amounted to only one thing. The reason I always carry a tin of that particular confectionery about my person is because, for parking-meter purposes, a Curiously Strong Peppermint is exactly the same size and weight as a 5p piece.

And that's why the encounter still retains a certain fragrance for me. Because even if it didn't exactly reach the status of a re-captured might-have-been, it did go part of the way towards achieving Mr Paley's ideal:

A triumph of mint over meter.